# Workshop on Language Technologies and Computational Social Science 2014



**Held at ACL 2014**

## Baltimore, Maryland, USA
## 26 June 2014

**ISBN: 978-1-63439-205-1**

**Printed from e-media with permission by:**

Curran Associates, Inc.
57 Morehouse Lane
Red Hook, NY 12571

**Some format issues inherent in the e-media version may also appear in this print version.**



Printed by Curran Associates, Inc. (2014)

For permission requests, please contact the Association for Computational Linguistics at the address below.

Association for Computational Linguistics
209 N. Eighth Street
Stroudsburg, Pennsylvania 18360

Phone: 1-570-476-8006
Fax: 1-570-476-0860

acl@aclweb.org

**Additional copies of this publication are available from:**

Curran Associates, Inc.
57 Morehouse Lane
Red Hook, NY 12571 USA
Phone: 845-758-0400
Fax: 845-758-2634
Email: curran@proceedings.com
Web: www.proceedings.com

# Preface

The ACL 2014 Workshop on Language Technologies and Computational Social Science was held on June 26, 2014 in Baltimore, following the 52nd annual meeting of the ACL. The workshop's goal was to increase the visibility of computational social science— in which automated techniques are applied to massive datasets to answer scientific questions about society—for ACL researchers and to help build connections between language technologists and social scientists.

The workshop included six invited talks from researchers who have successfully brought language technologies to computational social science research questions: political scientists Amber Boydstun and Justin Grimmer, social computing expert Ed Chi, sociolinguist Sali Tagliamonte, and computational linguists Lillian Lee and Philip Resnik.

Out of twenty submissions of short papers, thirteen were selected by the program committee for poster presentation. These represent an exciting, conversation-provoking range of research projects.

The workshop also included a session reporting on a related research competition, the NLP Unshared Task in PoliInformatics. A short overview paper is included in these proceedings.

This workshop was supported by grants from Google and the U.S. National Science Foudnation (grant IIS-1433108). These funds enabled the participation of the invited speakers, fourteen graduate students, and three more senior researchers.

We thank the invited speakers, program committee members, authors, and participants for sharing time and thoughts on this increasingly important research topic.

Cristian Danescu-Niculescu-Mizil, Jacob Eisenstein, Kathy McKeown, and Noah Smith

**Organizers:**

Cristian Danescu-Niculescu-Mizil, Max Planck Institute SWS
Jacob Eisenstein, Georgia Institute of Technology
Kathleen McKeown, Columbia University
Noah A. Smith, Carnegie Mellon University

**Program Committee:**

Jordan Boyd-Graber, University of Maryland
Claire Cardie, Cornell University
Munmun de Choudhury, Georgia Institute of Technology
Cindy Chung, University of Texas
Mark Dredze, Johns Hopkins University
Dan Jurafsky, Stanford University
Maria Liakata, University of Warwick
Brendan O'Connor, Carnegie Mellon University
Bo Pang, Google
Daniel Preoţiuc-Pietro, Sheffield University
Owen Rambow, Columbia University
Jaime Teevan, Microsoft
Hanna Wallach, University of Massachusetts

**Invited Speakers:**

Amber Boydstun, University of California at Davis
Ed Chi, Google
Justin Grimmer, Stanford University
Lillian Lee, Cornell University
Philip Resnik, University of Maryland
Sali Tagliamonte, University of Toronto

# Table of Contents

# Workshop Program

**Thursday, June 26, 2014**

| | |
|---|---|
| | **Welcome; Invited Talks, Style and Rhetoric** |
| 9:00 | Welcome |
| 9:05 | *Is It All in the Phrasing? Computational Explorations in How We Say What We Say, and Why It Matters*<br>Lillian Lee |
| 9:35 | *Creating and Destroying Party Brands*<br>Justin Grimmer |
| 10:05 | Discussion |
| | **(10:30-11:00) Coffee break** |
| | **Invited Talks, Sociolinguistics and Social Media** |
| 11:00 | *Sociolinguistics for Computational Social Science*<br>Sali Tagliamonte |
| 11:30 | *Location and Language Use in Social Media*<br>Ed Chi |
| 12:00 | Discussion |

**Thursday, June 26, 2014 (continued)**

**(12:30-2:00) Lunch break**

**(2:00-2:30) Unshared task**

2:00 *Overview of the 2014 NLP Unshared Task in PoliInformatics*
Noah A. Smith, Claire Cardie, Anne Washington and John Wilkerson

**(2:30-3:30) Poster session**

*Context-based Natural Language Processing for GIS-based Vague Region Visualization*
Wei Chen

*Extracting Socioeconomic Patterns from the News: Modelling Text and Outlet Importance Jointly*
Vasileios Lampos, Daniel Preoţiuc-Pietro, Sina Samangooei, Douwe Gelling and Trevor Cohn

*Fact Checking: Task definition and dataset construction*
Andreas Vlachos and Sebastian Riedel

*Finding Eyewitness Tweets During Crises*
Fred Morstatter, Nichola Lubold, Heather Pon-Barry, Jürgen Pfeffer and Huan Liu

*Inducing Information Structures for Data-driven Text Analysis*
Andrew Salway, Samia Touileb and Endre Tvinnereim

*Information density, Heaps' Law, and perception of factiness in news*
Miriam Boon

*Measuring the Public Accountability of New Modes of Governance*
Bruno Wueest, Gerold Schneider and Michael Amsler

*Optimizing Features in Active Machine Learning for Complex Qualitative Content Analysis*
Jasy Suet Yan Liew, Nancy McCracken, Shichun Zhou and Kevin Crowston

*Power of Confidence: How Poll Scores Impact Topic Dynamics in Political Debates*
Vinodkumar Prabhakaran, Ashima Arora and Owen Rambow

**Thursday, June 26, 2014 (continued)**

*Predicting Fine-grained Social Roles with Selectional Preferences*
Charley Beller, Craig Harman and Benjamin Van Durme

*Predicting Party Affiliations from European Parliament Debates*
Bjørn Høyland, Jean-François Godbout, Emanuele Lapponi and Erik Velldal

*Temporal Analysis of Language through Neural Language Models*
Yoon Kim, Yi-I Chiu, Kentaro Hanaki, Darshan Hegde and Slav Petrov

*Using Simple NLP Tools to Trace the Globalization of the Art World*
Mohamed AlTantawy, Alix Rule, Owen Rambow, Zhongyu Wang and Rupayan Basu

**(3:30-4:00) Coffee break**

**Invited Talks, Framing and Agenda-Setting**

4:00 *Issue Framing as a Generalizable Phenomenon*
Amber Boydstun

4:30 *"I Want to Talk About, Again, My Record On Energy ...": Modeling Agendas and Framing in Political Debates and Other Conversations*
Philip Resnik

5:00 Discussion

**(5:30) Closing remarks**

# Is It All in the Phrasing? Computational Explorations in How We Say What We Say, and Why It Matters

**Lillian Lee**
Cornell University

## Abstract

Louis Armstrong (is said to have) said, "I don't need words — it's all in the phrasing". As someone who does natural-language processing for a living, I'm a big fan of words; but lately, my collaborators and I have been studying aspects of phrasing (in the linguistic, rather than musical sense) that go beyond just the selection of one particular word over another. I'll describe some of these projects in this talk. The issues we'll consider include: Does the way in which something is worded in and of itself have an effect on whether it is remembered or attracts attention, beyond its content or context? Can we characterize how different sides in a debate frame their arguments, in a way that goes beyond specific lexical choice (e.g., "pro-choice" vs. "pro-life")? The settings we'll explore range from movie quotes that achieve cultural prominence; to posts on Facebook, Wikipedia, Twitter, and the arXiv; to framing in public discourse on the inclusion of genetically-modified organisms in food.

Joint work with Lars Backstrom, Justin Cheng, Eunsol Choi, Cristian Danescu-Niculescu-Mizil, Jon Kleinberg, Bo Pang, Jennifer Spindel, and Chenhao Tan.

## References

Lars Backstrom, Jon Kleinberg, Lillian Lee, and Cristian Danescu-Niculescu-Mizil. 2013. Characterizing and curating conversation threads: Expansion, focus, volume, re-entry. In *Proceedings of WSDM*, pages 13–22.

Eunsol Choi, Chenhao Tan, Lillian Lee, Cristian Danescu-Niculescu-Mizil, and Jennifer Spindel. 2012. Hedge detection as a lens on framing in the GMO debates: A position paper. In *Proceedings of the Workshop on Extra-Propositional Aspects of Meaning in Computational Linguistics*, pages 70–79.

Cristian Danescu-Niculescu-Mizil, Justin Cheng, Jon Kleinberg, and Lillian Lee. 2012. You had me at hello: How phrasing affects memorability. In *Proceedings of ACL*, pages 892–901.

Chenhao Tan and Lillian Lee. 2014. A corpus of sentence-level revisions in academic writing: A step towards understanding statement strength in communication. In *Proceedings of ACL (short paper)*.

Chenhao Tan, Lillian Lee, and Bo Pang. 2014. The effect of wording on message propagation: Topic- and author-controlled natural experiments on twitter. In *Proceedings of ACL*.



*Proceedings of the ACL 2014 Workshop on Language Technologies and Computational Social Science*, page 1,
Baltimore, Maryland, USA, June 26, 2014. 

# Creating and Destroying Party Brands

**Justin Grimmer**
Stanford University

## Abstract

Party brands are central to theories of Congressional action. While previous work assumes that a party's brand—its long run reputation—is a direct consequence of the content of legislation, in this presentation I show how partisans from both parties use public statements to craft their own party's reputation and to undermine their opponents party. The incentive to craft and destroy brands varies across legislators, creating systematic distortions in who contributes to partisan branding efforts, what is said about a party's brand, and when partisan criticism becomes salient. To demonstrate the construction of party brands I use new collections of newsletters from Congressional offices, along with press releases, floor speeches, and media broadcasts. Across the diverse sources, I show that ideologically extreme legislators are the most likely to explain their party's work in Washington and the most likely to criticize the opposing party—particularly when their is an opposing party president. Extreme legislators also engage in more vitriolic criticism of the opposing party, particularly when opposing presidents are unpopular. The result is that parties in rhetoric appear even more combative and polarized in public debate outside Congress than inside Congress.



*Proceedings of the ACL 2014 Workshop on Language Technologies and Computational Social Science*, page 2,
Baltimore, Maryland, USA, June 26, 2014. 

# Sociolinguistics for Computational Social Science

**Sali Tagliamonte**
University of Toronto

## Abstract

In recent years, a major growth area in applied natural language processing has been the application of automated techniques to massive datasets in order to answer questions about society, and by extension people. Sociolinguistics, which combines anthropology, statistics and linguistics (e.g. Labov 1994, 2001), studies linguistic data in order to answer key questions about the relationship of language and society. Sociolinguists focus on frequency and patterns in linguistic usage, correlations, strength of factors and significance, which together reveal information about the sex, age, education and occupation of speakers/writers but also their history, culture, place of residence, social relationships and affiliations. The findings arising from this type research offer important insights into the nature of human organizations at the global, national or community level. They also reveal connections and interactions, the convergence and divergence of groups, historical associations and developing trends.

In this paper, I will introduce sociolinguistic research and the nature of sociolinguistic field techniques and sample design. I will argue that socially embedded data is critical for analyzing and discovering social meaning. Then, I will summarize the findings of several case studies. What does the use of a 3rd singular morpheme -s, as in (1), tell us about the history and culture of a community (Tagliamonte 2012, 2013)? How is quotative be like, (2), spreading in geographic space (Tagliamonte to appear)? What is the mechanism that underlies linguistic change (Tagliamonte & D'Arcy 2009) and by extension cultural trends and projections?

1. The English people speaks with grammar.
2. I was *like*, "Hey how are you going?" And hes *like*, "Im fine."

Using sociolinguistic datasets, the answers to these questions have successfully addressed prevailing puzzles and offered solutions to real world problems. However this type of research is only be as good as the quality of the data, the capability of the technologies for extracting and analyzing what is important, and the relevance of the socially cogent and statistically sound interpretations. I will argue that Sociolinguists and Computational Scientists could be powerful allies in uncovering the complex structure of language data and in so doing, offer unsurpassed insight into varying human states and conditions.

## References

William Labov. 1994. *Principles of Linguistic Change: Volume 1: Internal Factors*. Blackwell.

William Labov. 2001. *Principles of Linguistic Change: Volume 2: Social Factors*. Blackwell.

Sali A. Tagliamonte and Alexandra D'Arcy. 2009. Peaks beyond phonology: Adolescence, incrementation, and language change. *Language*, 85(1):58–108.

Sali A. Tagliamonte. 2012. *Variationist Sociolinguistics: Change, Observation, Interpretation*. Wiley-Blackwell.

Sali A. Tagliamonte. 2013. *Roots of English: Exploring the History of Dialects*. Cambridge University Press.

Sali A. Tagliamonte. To appear. System and society in the evolution of change: The view from Canada. In E. Green and C. Meyer, editors, *Faces of English*. De Gruyter-Mouton.



*Proceedings of the ACL 2014 Workshop on Language Technologies and Computational Social Science*, page 3,
Baltimore, Maryland, USA, June 26, 2014. 

# Location and Language Use in Social Media

**Ed Chi**
Google

## Abstract

We now know that social interactions are critical in many knowledge and information processes. In this talk, I plan to illustrate a model-driven approach to understanding social behavior around user location and different languages in social media.

First, in 2010, we performed the first in-depth study of user location field in Twitter user profiles. We found that 34% of users did not provide real location information, frequently incorporating fake locations or sarcastic comments that can fool traditional geographic information tools. We then performed a simple machine learning experiment to determine whether we can identify a users location by only looking at contents of a user's tweets. We found that a users country and state can in fact be determined easily with decent accuracy, indicating that users implicitly reveal location information, with or without realizing it.

Second, despite the widespread adoption of Twitter in different locales, little research has investigated the differences among users of different languages. In prior research, the natural tendency has been to assume that the behaviors of English users generalize to other language users. We studied 62 million tweets collected over a four-week period. We discovered cross-language differences in adoption of features such as URLs, hashtags, mentions, replies, and retweets. We also found interesting patterns of how multi-lingual Twitter users broker information across these language boundaries. We discuss our works implications for research on large-scale social systems and design of cross-cultural communication tools.



*Proceedings of the ACL 2014 Workshop on Language Technologies and Computational Social Science*, page 4,
Baltimore, Maryland, USA, June 26, 2014. 

# Overview of the 2014 NLP Unshared Task in PoliInformatics

**Noah A. Smith*** **Claire Cardie†** **Anne L. Washington‡** **John D. Wilkerson§**
*School of Computer Science, Carnegie Mellon University, Pittsburgh, PA 15213, USA
†Department of Computer Science, Cornell University, Ithaca, NY 14853, USA
‡School of Public Policy, George Mason University, Arlington, VA 22201, USA
§Department of Political Science, University of Washington, Seattle, WA 98195, USA
*Corresponding author: nasmith@cs.cmu.edu

## Abstract

We describe a research activity carried out during January–April 2014, seeking to increase engagement between the natural language processing research community and social science scholars. In this activity, participants were offered a corpus of text relevant to the 2007–8 financial crisis and an open-ended prompt. Their responses took the form of a short paper and an optional demonstration, to which a panel of judges will respond with the goal of identifying efforts with the greatest potential for future interdisciplinary collaboration.

## 1 Introduction

In recent years, numerous interdisciplinary research meetings have sought to bring together computer scientists with expertise in automated text data analysis and scholars with substantive interests that might make use of text data. The latter group has included political scientists, economists, and communications scholars. An NSF Research Coordination Network grant to encourage research using open government data was awarded to co-authors Washington and Wilkerson in 2013. The network for Political Informatics, or PoliInformatics, brought together a steering committee from diverse research backgrounds that convened in February 2013. At that meeting, a substantive focus on the 2007–8 nancial crisis was selected.

Drawing inspiration from the "shared task" model that has been successful in the natural language processing community, we designed a research competition for computer scientists. In a shared task, a gold-standard dataset is created in advance of the competition, inputs and outputs are defined by the organizers, typically creating a supervised learning setup with held-out data used for evaluation. Constraints on the resources that may be used are typically set in place as well, to focus the energies of participants on a core problem, and the official evaluation scores are published, usually as open-source software. Final systems (or system output) is submitted by a deadline and judged automatically against the gold-standard. Participants report on their systems in short papers, typically presented at a meeting associated with a conference or workshop.

With neither a clear definition of what the final outcome might be, nor the resources to create the necessary gold-standard data, we developed a more open-ended competition. A text corpus was collected and made available, and a prompt was offered. Participants were given freedom in how to respond; competition entries took the form of short research papers and optional demonstrations of the results of the projects. Rather than an objective score, a panel of judges organized by the PoliInformatics steering committee offered public reviews of the work, with an emphasis on potential for future interdisciplinary research efforts that might stem from these preliminary projects.

## 2 Setup

The prompts offered to participants were:

**Who was the financial crisis?** We seek to understand the participants in the lawmaking and regulatory processes that formed the government's response to the crisis: the individuals, industries, and professionals targeted by those policies; the agencies and organizations responsible for implementing them; and the lobbyists, witnesses, advocates, and politicians who were actively involved—and the connections among them.

**What was the financial crisis?** We seek to understand the cause(s) of the crisis, proposals for reform, advocates for those proposals, arguments



*Proceedings of the ACL 2014 Workshop on Language Technologies and Computational Social Science*, pages 5–7,
Baltimore, Maryland, USA, June 26, 2014. 

for and against, policies ultimately adopted by the government, and the impact of those policies.

The set of datasets made available is listed in Table 1. Several additional datasets were suggested on the website,[1] but were not part of the official data.

## 3 Response

Forty teams initially registered to participate in the unshared task; ten submitted papers. The teams came from a variety of institutions spread across six countries. Half of the teams included links to online demonstrations or browsable system output. At this writing, the papers are under review by the panel of judges. We provide a very brief summary of the contributions of each team.

### 3.1 Who was the financial crisis?

Bordea et al. (2014) inferred importance and hierarchy of topics along with expertise mining to find which participants in the discourse might be experts (e.g., Paul Volcker and "proprietary trading") based on FOMC, FCIC, and Congressional hearing and report data.

Baerg et al. (2014) considered transcripts of the FOMC, developing a method for scaling the preferences of its members with respect to inflation (hawks to doves); the method incorporates automatic dimensionality reduction and expert topic interpretation.

Zirn et al. (2014) also focused on the transcripts, distinguishing between position-taking statements and shorter "discussion elements" that express agreement or disagreement rather than substance, and used this analysis to quantify similarity among FOMC members and take first steps toward extraction of sub-dialogues among them.

Bourreau and Poibeau (2014) focused on the FCIC report and the two Congressional reports, identifying named entities and then visualizing correlations among mentions both statically (as networks) and dynamically. Clark et al. (2014) considered Congressional hearings, applying a reasoning model that integrates analysis of social roles and relationships with analysis of individual beliefs in hope of detecting opinion shifts and signs of influence.

With an eye toward substantive hypotheses about dependencies among banks' access to bailout funds relating to underlying social connections, Morales et al. (2014) automatically extracted a social network from the corpus alongside structured data in Freebase.

### 3.2 What was the financial crisis?

Miller and McCoy (2014) considered FOMC transcripts, applying topic models for dimensionality reduction and viewing topic proportions as time series.

In a study of the TARP, Dodd-Frank, and the health reform bills, Li et al. (2014) explored the ideas expressed in those bills, applying models of text reuse from bills introduced in the 110th and 111th Congresses.

Wang et al. (2014) implemented a query-focused summarization system for FOMC and FCIC meeting transcripts and Congressional hearings, incorporating topic and expertise measures into the score, and queried the corpus with candidate causes for the crisis, derived from Wikipedia (e.g., "subprime lending" and "growth housing bubble").

Kleinnijenhuis et al. (2014) considered Congressional hearings alongside news text from the United States and the United Kingdom, carrying out keyword analysis to compare and measure directional effects between the two, on different dimensions.

## 4 Conclusion

The unshared task was successful in attracting the interest of forty participants working on ten teams. A highly diverse range of activities ensued, each of which is being reviewed at this writing by a panel of judges. Reviews and final outcomes will be posted at the `https://sites.google.com/site/unsharedtask2014` as soon as they are available, and a presentation summarizing the competition will be part of the ACL 2014 Workshop on Language Technologies and Computational Social Science.

## Acknowledgments

We thank the participants and judges for their time and effort. This activity was supported in part by NSF grants 1243917 and 1054319.

[1] `https://sites.google.com/site/unsharedtask2014`

- Federal Open Market Committee (FOMC):
  - Meeting transcripts are only made available five years after each meeting date. (The 2008 transcripts came available around the time of the activity and were kindly made available by participant William Li.)
  - Meeting minutes are available for all meetings to date.
- Federal Crisis Inquiry Commission (FCIC; an independent commission created by Congress to investigate the causes of the crisis):
  - Report
  - Transcript of the first public hearing
- Congressional reports:
  - Senate Committee on Homeland Security and Governmental Affairs: "Wall Street and the financial crisis: anatomy of a financial collapse"
  - House Committee on Financial Services: "The stock market plunge: what happened and what is next?"
- Congressional bills:
  - Troubled Assets Relief Program, 2008 (TARP)
  - Dodd-Frank Wall Street Reform and Consumer Protection Act (2010)
  - American Recovery and Reinvestment Act of 2009 (Stimulus)
  - Housing and Economic Recovery Act of 2008
  - Public Company Accounting Reform and Investor Protection Act of 2002 (Sarbanes-Oxley)
  - Financial Services Modernization Act of 1999 (Gramm-Leach-Bliley)
  - In addition to the above financial reform bills, the text of all versions of all Congressional bills introduced in the 110th and 111th Congresses
- Congressional hearings, segmented into turns:
  - Monetary policy (26)
  - TARP (12)
  - Dodd-Frank (61)
  - Other selected committee hearings relating to financial reform (15)

Table 1: Text datasets made available to unshared task participants. These can be downloaded at `https://sites.google.com/site/unsharedtask2014`.

## References


Nicole Rae Baerg, Will Lowe, Simone Ponzetto, Heiner Stuckenschmidt, and Căcilia Zirn. 2014. Estimating central bank preferences.

Georgeta Bordea, Kartik Asooja, Paul Buitelaar, and Leona O'Brien. 2014. Gaining insights into the global financial crisis using Saffron.

Pierre Bourreau and Thierry Poibeau. 2014. Mapping the economic crisis: Some preliminary investigations.

Micah Clark, Adam Dalton, Tomas By, Yorick Wilks, Samira Shaikh, Ching-Sheng Lin, and Tomek Strzalkowski. 2014. Influence and belief in Congressional hearings.

Jan Kleinnijenhuis, Wouter van Atteveldt, and Antske Fokkens. 2014. Chicken or egg? the reciprocal influence of press and politics.

William P. Li, David Larochelle, and Andrew W. Lo. 2014. Estimating policy trajectories during the financial crisis.

John E. Miller and Kathleen F. McCoy. 2014. Changing focus of the FOMC through the financial crisis.

Michelle Morales, David Brizan, Hussein Ghaly, Thomas Hauner, Min Ma, and Andrew Rosenberg. 2014. Application of social network analysis in the estimation of bank financial strength during the financial crisis.

Lu Wang, Parvaz Mahdabi, Joonsuk Park, Dinesh Puranam, Bishan Yang, and Claire Cardie. 2014. Cornell expert aided query-focused summarization (CEAQS): A summarization framework to PoliInformatics.

Căcilia Zirn, Michael Schäfer, Simone Paolo Ponzetto, and Michael Strube. 2014. Exploring structural features for position analysis in political discussions.

# Context-based Natural Language Processing for GIS-based Vague Region Visualization

[1,2]Wei Chen
[1]Department of Computer Science and Engineering, [2]Department of Geography
The Ohio State University, Columbus OH, USA 43210
chen.1381@osu.edu

## Abstract

Vernacular regions such as *central Ohio* are popularly used in everyday language; but their vague and indeterministic boundaries affect the clarity of communicating them over the geographic space. This paper introduced a context-based natural language processing approach to retrieve geographic entities. Geographic entities extracted from news articles were used as location-based behavioral samples to map out the vague region of *central Ohio*. Particularly, part of speech tagging and parse tree generation were employed to filter out candidate entities from English sentences. Propositional logic of context (PLC) was introduced and adapted to build the contextual model for deciding the membership of named entities. Results were automatically generated and visualized in GIS using both symbol and density mapping. Final maps were consistent with our intuition and common sense knowledge of the vague region.

## 1 Introduction

*Central Ohio* is commonly used vernacular term to refer to an approximate area around the city of Columbus in Ohio. Although it may be effortless for humans to tell the relative location of this region, it remains challenging for computers to automatically locate this region by harvesting and analyzing online data such as news articles. Computers that are capable of automatically delineating such vague regions may be of potential use to social science researchers for understanding other concepts that may not be as obvious such as cultural regions, *the Muslim world.*

In the study of vague regions, previous studies introduced a behavioral method to map out downtown Santa Barbara based on human survey data (Montello, Goodchild, Gottsegen, & Fohl, 2003). Their approach collected hand-drawn point-based locations and plotted them on the map of the city. Such data collection process may be very costly compared to computer-based automated approach. By comparison, natural language processing (NLP) techniques such as part of speech tagging and parse tree generation provide powerful linguistic analysis tools that can help quickly retrieve data from a large number of corpus data (Jurafsky, Martin, Kehler, Vander Linden, & Ward, 2000). However, these NLP techniques have yet been widely used to extract geographic entities for visualizing vague regions like *central Ohio*.

On the other hand, linguistic contexts of named entities are important for deciding its relevancy to the underlying vague regions. For instance, for a place to be part of *central Ohio*, it must be in the context of Ohio as a precondition. Propositional logic of context (PLC) is a logic model in the field of artificial intelligence for formalizing contexts into propositional calculus (BuvaE & Mason, 1993). Based on PLC, an arbitrary predicate calculus can be evaluated according to selected contexts.

In this paper, *central Ohio* is chosen as the experimental area to experiment the context-based natural language approach for visualizing vague regions. News articles are used and analyzed on three contextual levels: document, paragraph and sentence. Results are visualized in GIS.

### 1.1 News data

News articles are extracted from LexisNexis, a comprehensive database of both national and local news (Smith, Ellenberg, Bell, & Rubin, 2008). All articles are retrieved based on caseless keyword match for relevancy. The only keyword used is *central Ohio* and only news articles that contain this exact phrase are retrieved. As a result, 3281 different articles are collected which cover central Ohio news from the year 1990 to the year 2013.



*Proceedings of the ACL 2014 Workshop on Language Technologies and Computational Social Science*, pages 8–12,
Baltimore, Maryland, USA, June 26, 2014. ©2014 Association for Computational Linguistics

### 1.2 Geonames database

Geonames database contains names and locations of geographic entities. We create our geonames database two sources: the United States Geological Survey's Geographic Names
Information Server (USGS, 2013) and Census gazetteers (Census, 2013). Only place and feature names in Ohio used for analysis. Table 1 summarizes compositions of entities in our Ohio geonames database.

| Category | Percentages |
|---|---|
| Administrative places (1054 records) | 23.0% cities<br>66.3% villages<br>10.6% CDPs (census designated place) |
| Geographic features (67804 records) | 14.9% church<br>13.7% school<br>12.6% populated place among 53 categories |

Table 1. Geographic named entities in Ohio

## 2 Natural Language Processing

Part of speech tagging and parse tree generation are used to automatically extract geographic named entities from news articles in this paper. Part of speech (POS) tagging is the process of deciding the functions of words such as nouns or verbs. Parse tree generation is based on POS tagging results. It aims to generate hierarchical representations of sentences for semantic understanding (Jurafsky et al., 2000). Noun phrases in the parse tree are often useful indicators to named entities in geolinguistic analysis (Chen et al., 2013).

### 2.1 Part of speech tagging

Part-of-speech (POS) tagging assigns a POS tag to each token in a sentence. A token can be either a word or a punctuation. The single best POS tag assigned to a token depends on the function of the word, the tag set, and POS tagging algorithm (Jurafsky et al., 2000). Contemporary POS taggers can reach an average accuracy of above 97% on tokens (Manning, 2011).

The part of speech tagger we use is Stanford NLP tagger with english-caseless-left3words-distsim tagger model. This tagger model is trained with WSJ sections 0-18 and extra parser training data using the left3words architecture. It includes word shape and distributional similarity features for training the tagger (Gimpel et al., 2010). The results are represented using Penn Treebank tags and the average parsing accuracy is above 97% on sentences in news. Box 1 is the tagged sentence from one article with POS tags appended after the slash in uppercase letters. For a complete list, one may refer to Penn Treebank tag sets.

> Her/PRP$ friends/NNS at/IN the/DT Central/NNP Ohio/NNP Nazarene/NNP Church/NNP Camp/NNP she/PRP attended/VBD every/DT summer/NN in/IN Columbus/NNP convinced/VBD her/PRP to/TO attend/VB Mount/NNP Vernon/NNP Nazarene/NNP College/NNP in/IN Knox/JJ county/NN ,/, OH/NNP ./.

Box 1. Tagged sentence

### 2.2 Parsing

Stanford parsers are used to produce the parse tree from which noun phrases, named entity candidates, can be extracted (De Marneffe, MacCartney, & Manning, 2006) . Fig.1 shows the result of parsing the tagged sentence in Box 1. It is observed that only noun phrases (NP) at the lowest level of the tree are useful for extracting named entities. Noun phrases at other levels contain auxiliary structures such as prepositions often do not suggest named entities.

In Fig.1, NPs in dashed rectangles are candidate entities that do not match any records in our Ohio database. When looking up the database for a match, determinants like *the* are skipped as well as entity type terms like *city* and *county*. To find the location of a matched entity, a SQL query is used to return the latitude and longitude pair.

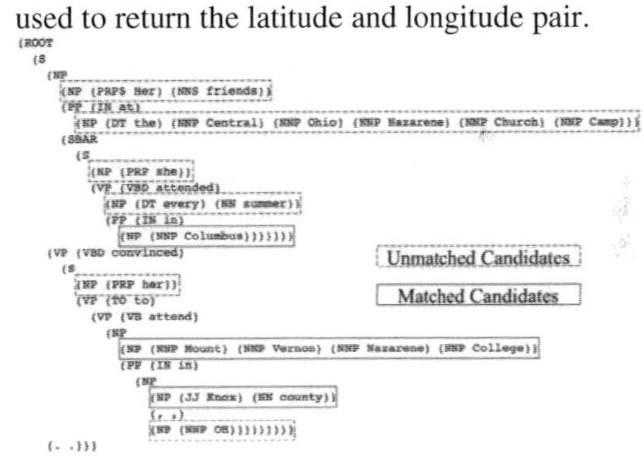


Figure 1. Parse tree of tagged sentence in Box 1

## 3 Geographic Information Retrieval

### 3.1 Propositional logic of context (PLC)

As previously discussed, candidate named entities are primarily noun phrases extracted at the root level of a parse tree. However, not all such entities should be considered as part of central Ohio. To determine the membership, we may define following logic heuristics: if (1) the name of an entity is in the same text segment as the phrase *central Ohio* and (2) the entity is an Ohio place, then the entity is of greater likelihood of being a central Ohio place than otherwise. Here, Ohio and central

Ohio are linguistic contexts for discriminating central Ohio entities.

To formalize the contexts of analysis, we introduce propositional logic of context (PLC) (BuvaE & Mason, 1993). Here, we only adapt its basic form as it already suffice the needs of our analysis. For detailed information of PLC, one may read the original paper from BuvaE (BuvaE & Mason, 1993). The minimum PLC definition is below:

x: subject
p: preposition about the subject
c: context
$c_1 \wedge c_2$: logic AND, intersection of two contexts
$c_1 \vee c_2$: logic OR, union of two contexts
ist(c, p): the proposition p is true in context c.

### 3.2 PLC-based matching and counting

Based on the PLC definition, we count the mentions of named entities in all news articles. Here, we define the following PLC notations for our analysis:

p: the preposition that x is a central Ohio city
$c_1$: the context of Ohio
$c_2$: the context of central Ohio
$c_3$: the context of not-central Ohio

Ohio context is defined according to records in geonames database. If an entity name is in the database, it is said to be in the Ohio context. Central Ohio context is defined as the text segment containing both the entity name and the phrase *central Ohio*. Not-central Ohio context is defined as the text segment with the following terms in it: *north(ern) Ohio*, *northeast(ern) Ohio*, *east(ern) Ohio*, *southeast(ern) Ohio*, *south(ern) Ohio*, *southwest(ern) Ohio*, *west(ern) Ohio*, and *northwest(ern) Ohio*. Based on our observation, these eight azimuth phrases are found to be good indicators of places that are obviously not in central Ohio.

Accordingly, three types of entity counts are also developed.

(1) *Positive count (E)*: the total number of occurrences of the name of an entity E in the context $c_1 \wedge c_2$.
(2) *Neutral count* (E): the total number of occurrences of the name of an entity E in the context $c_1 \wedge \neg c_2 \wedge \neg c_3$.
(3) *Negative count (E)*: the total number of occurrences of the name of an entity E in the context $c_1 \wedge c_3$.

### 3.3 Count and normalization

We calculate the membership of an entity to the concept *central Ohio* using following counting and normalization rules. We define three variables to count entity occurrences in different contexts:

$C_{pos}$ : positive count of the entity E.
$C_{neg}$ : negative count of the entity E.
$C_{neu}$ : neutral count of the entity E.
IF ist($c_1 \wedge c_2$, p), $C_{pos}$++.
IF ist($c_1 \wedge c_3$, p), $C_{neg}$++.
IF ist($c_1 \wedge \neg c_2 \wedge \neg c_3$, p), $C_{neu}$++.

Based on observations, big cities like *Columbus* are mentioned more frequently than other smaller places in term of both $C_{pos}$ and $C_{neg}$. As it is the difference between $C_{pos}$ and $C_{neg}$ that determines the sign of the membership, we decide to use $C_{neu}$ as the normalization denominator for calculating the membership.

Membership *r* of a place is calculated using Equation 1. It is a real value between -1 and 1. All places are classified by the sign of the membership as either *central Ohio* or *not-central Ohio* place with the magnitude of the value being the strength of the membership. 1 means definitely a central Ohio place and -1 means definitely not a central Ohio place.

$$r = \begin{cases} (C_{pos} - C_{neg})/C_{neu} & \text{, if } C_{neu} > 0 \\ 0 & \text{, otherwise} \end{cases} \quad Equation\ 1$$

As $C_{neu}$ is in the denominator, it must not be zero. Given observations, entities with $C_{neu}$ being zero are primarily entities with less than 3 total mentions. These entities take up 3.9% of all extracted entities. Therefore, we decide to exclude them from analysis as they are of a small percentage and are not expected to affect the overall results.

## 4 Results and discussions

Geographic entities are extracted from all 3281 news articles and their membership values are mapped using the geographic information system (GIS) software ArcGIS which are popular in social science geographic research.

### 4.1 Graduated symbol maps

Graduated symbol map is a type of map that uses symbols of different sizes to represent geographic entities (Thrall, 1999). The symbol we choose is circle. The radius of the circle is decided by the attribute value associated with each entity. The map is configured as follows:

(1) The size of each point is proportioned to the membership of the underlying named entity with size 4 and 24 representing the minimum and maximum membership respectively.
(2) Symbols are classified into 10 classes based on equal interval classification method.

There is one exception of using the membership for making the graduated symbol map. On the article level, all entity counts are added to $C_{pos}$, and therefore there are no negative or neutral counts. To make a map on the article level, we only use the positive count as the surrogate to the membership value.

Graduated symbol maps on three analytical levels are shown in Fig. 2. Results on the sentence level and paragraph levels conforms better to our intuition and common sense knowledge than on the article level. This is because results on the article level do not consider the contexts of $c_1$ and $c_2$ discussed in section 4.2. Results from the sentence and paragraph levels are very similar with the membership on the paragraph level being slightly more visually significant.

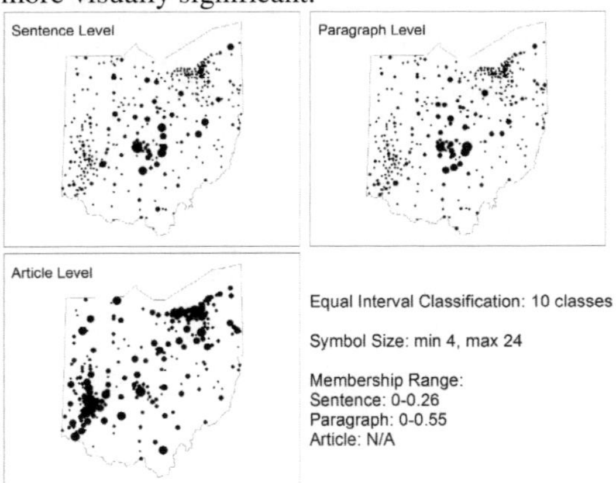


Figure 2. Graduated symbol map of central Ohio

### 4.2 Kernel density map

Results produced by graduated symbol maps are not continuous. Kernel density mapping is a GIS mapping technique that generates a continuous surface based on the locations of the entities and their attribute values (Elgammal, Duraiswami, Harwood, & Davis, 2002). To create kernel density maps, a search radius need be defined. All data points within this radius will be used to interpolate a density area using a quadratic kernel function described in Silverman (p. 76, equation 4.5) (Silverman, 1986).

The kernel density tool in ArcGIS is used to create the density map. In ArcGIS, the search radius is defined as a percentage of the area's minimum extent width. We experiment on choosing 1/10, 1/5, 1/20 of the area's minimum extent width as the radius to generate the surface and find 1/10 of the width most appropriate to generate a balanced looking map.

A kernel density map of *central Ohio* visualizes its estimated central location and extending trend over the space of Ohio. Fig. 3 is a kernel density result based on the paragraph level. It shows that the concept of central Ohio generated through automated approach conforms to our common sense knowledge of the assumptive location of the vague region.

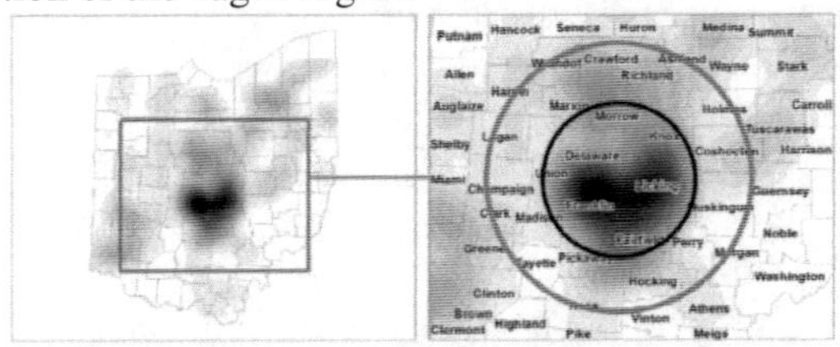

Figure 3. Kernel density map of central Ohio

## 5 Conclusions

Vague geographic regions are important part of the entire geographic space; however they are difficult to be located and delineated on a map. Geographic questions like *Where is central Ohio?* remains a challenge to computers because computers are not automatically given the knowledge of either *central* or *Ohio* as humans do.

This paper introduced a context-based approach to extract geographic entities from news articles. Propositional logic of context was adapted to contextualize the reasoning process. Three types of context have been defined: *Ohio*, *central Ohio*, *not-central Ohio*, which corresponded to *Ohio places*, *central Ohio places* and *not-central Ohio places*, respectively.

Analysis was conducted on three contextual levels: *article*, *paragraph* and *sentence*. Visualization results showed that context was of significant importance to deciding the membership of a place to *central Ohio*. Without defining the context (e.g. results on the article level in Fig. 2), visualization results were largely incorrect compared with common sense knowledge.

Natural language processing (NLP) techniques such as part of speech tagging and parse tree generation were shown to be effective for extracting geographic information. Noun phrases could serve as good candidates to place names. For future research, we suggest studies on experimenting with different regional concepts using proposed approach. It may also be useful to experiment with methods that can quickly generate samples other than the tree parsing method used in this paper. Despite the possibility of generating more coarse results, noisier method may be more scalable for building practical applications with scaled live data.

## Acknowledgements

The author would like to thank Dr. Xiang Chen, Dr. Zhe Xu, Dr. Lili Wang, Dr. Xueying Zhang, Dr. Bo Zhao, Dr. Ningchuan Xiao and two other anonymous reviewers for their valuable comments and suggestions for improving the paper. Presentation of the work was supported by the research data and computing center of the research institute at the Nationwide Children's Hospital.

## Reference

BuvaE, Saga, & Mason, Ian A. (1993). *Propositional logic of context.* Paper presented at the Proceedings of the eleventh national conference on artificial intelligence.

Census. (2013). U.S. Gazetteer Files. from http://www.census.gov/geo/www/gazetteer/files/Gaz_places_national.txt

Chen, Wei, Fosler-Lussier, Eric, Xiao, Ningchuan, Raje, Satyajeet, Ramnath, Rajiv, & Sui, Daniel. (2013). *A Synergistic Framework for Geographic Question Answering.* Paper presented at the Semantic Computing (ICSC), 2013 IEEE Seventh International Conference on.

De Marneffe, Marie-Catherine, MacCartney, Bill, & Manning, Christopher D. (2006). *Generating typed dependency parses from phrase structure parses.* Paper presented at the Proceedings of LREC.

Elgammal, Ahmed, Duraiswami, Ramani, Harwood, David, & Davis, Larry S. (2002). Background and foreground modeling using nonparametric kernel density estimation for visual surveillance. *Proceedings of the IEEE, 90*(7), 1151-1163.

Gimpel, Kevin, Schneider, Nathan, O'Connor, Brendan, Das, Dipanjan, Mills, Daniel, Eisenstein, Jacob, . . . Smith, Noah A. (2010). Part-of-speech tagging for twitter: Annotation, features, and experiments: DTIC Document.

Jurafsky, Dan, Martin, James H, Kehler, Andrew, Vander Linden, Keith, & Ward, Nigel. (2000). *Speech and language processing: An introduction to natural language processing, computational linguistics, and speech recognition* (Vol. 2): MIT Press.

Manning, Christopher D. (2011). Part-of-speech tagging from 97% to 100%: is it time for some linguistics? *Computational Linguistics and Intelligent Text Processing* (pp. 171-189): Springer.

Montello, Daniel R, Goodchild, Michael F, Gottsegen, Jonathon, & Fohl, Peter. (2003). Where's downtown?: Behavioral methods for determining referents of vague spatial queries. *Spatial Cognition & Computation, 3*(2-3), 185-204.

Silverman, Bernard W. (1986). *Density estimation for statistics and data analysis* (Vol. 26): CRC press.

Smith, Michael J, Ellenberg, Susan S, Bell, Louis M, & Rubin, David M. (2008). Media coverage of the measles-mumps-rubella vaccine and autism controversy and its relationship to MMR immunization rates in the United States. *Pediatrics, 121*(4), e836-e843.

Thrall, Susan Elshaw. (1999). Geographic information system (GIS) hardware and software. *Journal of Public Health Management and Practice, 5*(2), 82&hyhen.

USGS. (2013). Geographic Names Information Server. from http://geonames.usgs.gov/index.html

# Extracting Socioeconomic Patterns from the News: Modelling Text and Outlet Importance Jointly

**Vasileios Lampos[1], Daniel Preoţiuc-Pietro[2], Sina Samangooei[3], Douwe Gelling[2], and Trevor Cohn[4]**

[1] Department of Computer Science, University College London — v.lampos@ucl.ac.uk

[2] Department of Computer Science, The University of Sheffield — {d.preotiuc,d.gelling}@shef.ac.uk

[3] Electronics and Computer Science, University of Southampton — ss@ecs.soton.ac.uk

[4] Computing and Information Systems, The University of Melbourne — t.cohn@unimelb.edu.au

## Abstract

Information from news articles can be used to study correlations between textual discourse and socioeconomic patterns. This work focuses on the task of understanding how words contained in the news as well as the news outlets themselves may relate to a set of indicators, such as economic sentiment or unemployment rates. The bilinear nature of the applied regression model facilitates learning jointly word and outlet importance, supervised by these indicators. By evaluating the predictive ability of the extracted features, we can also assess their relevance to the target socioeconomic phenomena. Therefore, our approach can be formulated as a potential NLP tool, particularly suitable to the computational social science community, as it can be used to interpret connections between vast amounts of textual content and measurable society-driven factors.

## 1 Introduction

Vast amounts of user-generated content on the Internet as well as digitised textual resources allow us to study text in connection to real world events across large intervals of time. Over the last decade, there has been a shift in user news consumption starting with a move from offline to online sources (Lin et al., 2005); in more recent years user-generated news have also become prominent. However, traditional news outlets continue to be a central reference point (Nah and Chung, 2012) as they still have the advantage of being professionally authored, alleviating the noisy nature of citizen journalism formats.

Here, we present a framework for analysing socioeconomic patterns in news articles. In contrast to prior approaches, which primarily focus on the textual contents, our analysis shows how Machine Learning methods can be used to gain insights into the interplay between text in news articles, the news outlets and socioeconomic indicators. Our experiments are performed on a set of EU-related news summaries spanning over 8 years, with the intention to study two basic economic factors: EU's unemployment rate and Economic Sentiment Index (ESI) (European Commision, 1997). To determine connections between the news, the outlets and the indicators of interest, we formulate our learning task as bilinear text-based regression (Lampos et al., 2013).

Approaches to learning the correlation of news, or text in general, with real world indicators have been performed in both unsupervised and supervised settings. For example, Flaounas et al. (2010) uncover interesting patterns in EU's Mediasphere, whereas Schumaker and Chen (2009) demonstrate that news articles can predict financial indicators. Conversely, Bentley et al. (2014) show that emotions in the textual content of books reflect back on inflation and unemployment rates during the 20th century. Recently, Social Media text has been intensively studied as a quicker, unobtrusive and cheaper alternative to traditional surveys. Application areas include politics (O'Connor et al., 2010), finance (Bollen and Mao, 2011), health (Lampos and Cristianini, 2012; Paul and Dredze, 2011) or psychology (De Choudhury et al., 2013; Schwartz et al., 2013).

In this paper, we apply a modified version of a bilinear regularised regression model (BEN) proposed for the task of voting intention inference from Twitter content (Lampos et al., 2013). The main characteristic of BEN is the ability of modelling word frequencies as well as individual user importance in a joint optimisation task. By applying it in the context of supervised news analysis, we are able to visualise relevant discourse to a particular socioeconomic factor, identifying relevant words together with important outlets.



*Proceedings of the ACL 2014 Workshop on Language Technologies and Computational Social Science*, pages 13–17, Baltimore, Maryland, USA, June 26, 2014. 

## 2 Data

We compiled a data set by crawling summaries on news articles written in English language, published by the Open Europe Think Tank.[1] The press summaries are daily aggregations of news items about the EU or member countries with a focus on politics; the news outlets used to compile each summary are listed below the summary's text. The site is updated every weekday, with the major news being covered in a couple of paragraphs, and other less prevalent issues being mentioned in one paragraph to as little as one sentence. The news summaries were first published on February 2006; we collected all of them up to mid-November 2013, creating a data set with the temporal resolution of 1913 days (or 94 months).

The text was tokenised using the NLTK library (Bird et al., 2009). News outlets with fewer than 5 mentions were removed, resulting in a total of 435 sources. Each summary contains on average 14 news items, with an average of 3 news sources per item; where multiple sources were present, the summary was assigned to all the referenced news outlets. After removing stop words, we ended up with 8,413 unigrams and 19,045 bigrams; their daily occurrences were normalised using the total number of news items for that day.

For the purposes of our supervised analysis, we use the response variables of ESI and unemployment rate across the EU. The monthly time series of these socioeconomic indicators were retrieved from Eurostat, EU's statistical office (see the red lines in Fig. 1a and 1b respectively). ESI is a composite indicator often seen as an early predictor for future economic developments (Gelper and Croux, 2010). It consists of five confidence indicators with different weights: industrial (40%), services (30%), consumer (20%), construction (5%) and retail trade (5%). The unemployment rate is a seasonally adjusted ratio of the non employed persons over the entire EU labour force.[2]

## 3 Models

A common approach to regression arises through the application of generalised linear models. These models use a feature vector input $\boldsymbol{x}$ and aim to build a linear function of $\boldsymbol{x}$ for predicting a response variable $y$:

$$f(\boldsymbol{x}) = \boldsymbol{x}^{\mathrm{T}}\boldsymbol{w} + \beta \quad \text{where } \boldsymbol{x}, \boldsymbol{w} \in \mathbb{R}^m. \quad (1)$$

The objective is to find an $f$, which minimises a model-dependent loss function (e.g. sum squared error), optionally subject to a regularisation penalty $\psi$; $\ell_2$-norm regularisation (ridge regression) penalises high weights (Hoerl and Kennard, 1970), while $\ell_1$-norm regularisation (lasso) encourages sparse solutions (Tibshirani, 1994). Sparsity is desirable for avoiding overfitting, especially when the dimensionality $m$ is larger than the number of training examples $n$ (Hastie et al., 2009). Elastic Net formulates a combination of $\ell_1$ and $\ell_2$-norm regularisation defined by the objective:

$$\begin{aligned}\{\boldsymbol{w}^*, \beta^*\} = \underset{\boldsymbol{w},\beta}{\operatorname{argmin}} \sum_{i=1}^{n} (\boldsymbol{x}_i^{\mathrm{T}} \cdot \boldsymbol{w} + \beta - y_i)^2 \\ + \psi_{\mathrm{EN}}(\boldsymbol{w}, \rho)\,,\end{aligned} \quad (2)$$

where $\rho$ denotes the regularisation parameters (Zou and Hastie, 2005); we refer to this model as **LEN** (Linear Elastic Net) in the remainder of the script.

In the context of voting intention inference from Twitter content, Lampos et al. (2013) extended LEN to a bilinear formulation, where a set of two vector weights are learnt: one for words ($\boldsymbol{w}$) and one for users ($\boldsymbol{u}$). This was motivated by the observation that only a sparse set of users may have predictive value. The model now becomes:

$$f(X) = \boldsymbol{u}^{\mathrm{T}} X \boldsymbol{w} + \beta\,, \quad (3)$$

where $X$ is a matrix of word $\times$ users frequencies. The bilinear optimisation objective is formulated as:

$$\begin{aligned}\{\boldsymbol{w}^*, \boldsymbol{u}^*, \beta^*\} = \underset{\boldsymbol{w},\boldsymbol{u},\beta}{\operatorname{argmin}} \sum_{i=1}^{n} \left(\boldsymbol{u}^{\mathrm{T}} X_i \boldsymbol{w} + \beta - y_i\right)^2 \\ + \psi_{\mathrm{EN}}(\boldsymbol{w}, \rho_1) + \psi_{\mathrm{EN}}(\boldsymbol{u}, \rho_2)\,,\end{aligned} \quad (4)$$

where $X_i$ is the word $\times$ user frequency matrix, and $\rho_1, \rho_2$ are the word and user regularisation parameters. This can be treated as a biconvex learning task and be solved by iterating over two convex processes: fixing $\boldsymbol{w}$ and learning $\boldsymbol{u}$, and vice versa (Lampos et al., 2013). Regularised regression on both user and word spaces allows for an automatic selection of the most important words and users, performing at the same time an improved noise filtering.

[1] http://www.openeurope.org.uk/Page/PressSummary/en/

[2] http://epp.eurostat.ec.europa.eu/statistics_explained/index.php/Unemployment_statistics

In our experiments, news outlets and socioeconomic indicators replace users and voting intention in the previous model formulation. To ease the interpretation of the outputs, we further impose a positivity constraint on the outlet weights $\boldsymbol{u}$, i.e. $\min(\boldsymbol{u}) \geq 0$; this makes the model more restrictive, but, in our case, did not affect the prediction performance. We refer to this model as **BEN** (Bilinear Elastic Net).

## 4 Experiments

Both models are applied to the news summaries data set with the aim to predict EU's ESI and rate of unemployment. The predictive capability of the derived models, assessed by their respective inference performance, is used as a metric for judging the degree of relevance between the learnt model parameters – word and outlet weights – and the response variable. A strong predictive performance increases confidence on the soundness of those parameters.

To match input with the monthly temporal resolution of the response variables, we compute the mean monthly term frequencies for each outlet. Evaluation is performed via a 10-fold validation, where each fold's training set is based on a moving window of $p = 64$ contiguous months, and the test set consists of the following $q = 3$ months; formally, the training and test sets for fold $i$ are based on months $\{q(i-1)+1, ..., q(i-1)+p\}$ and $\{q(i-1)+p+1, ..., q(i-1)+p+q\}$ respectively. In this way, we emulate a scenario where we always train on past and predict future points.

Performance results for LEN and BEN are presented in Table 1; we show the average Root Mean Squared Error (RMSE) as well as an error rate (RMSE over $\mu(y)$) across folds to allow for a better interpretation. BEN outperforms LEN in both tasks, with a clearer improvement when predicting ESI. Predictions for all folds are depicted in Fig. 1a and 1b together with the actual values. Note that reformulating the problem into a multi-task learning scenario, where ESI and unemployment are modelled jointly did not improve inference performance.

The relatively small average error rates ($< 8.8\%$) make meaningful a further analysis of the model's outputs. Due to space limitations, we choose to focus on the most recent results, depicting the models derived in the 10th fold. Following the example of Schwartz et al. (2013), we use a word cloud visu-

| | ESI | Unemployment |
|---|---|---|
| **LEN** | 9.253 (9.89%) | 0.9275 (8.75%) |
| **BEN** | **8.209** (8.77%) | **0.9047** (8.52%) |

Table 1: 10-fold validation average RMSEs (and error rates) for LEN and BEN on ESI and unemployment rates prediction.

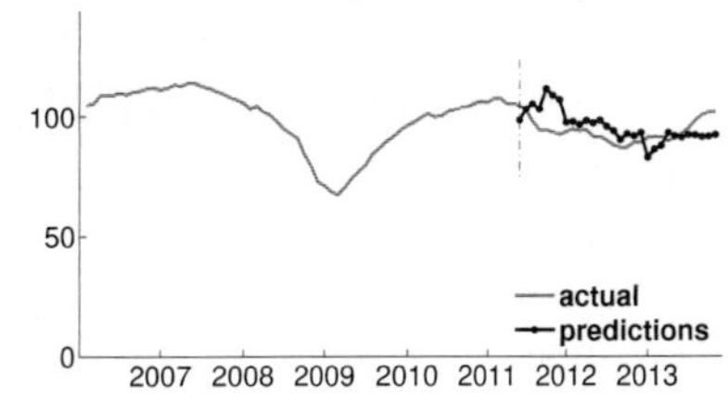


(a) ESI

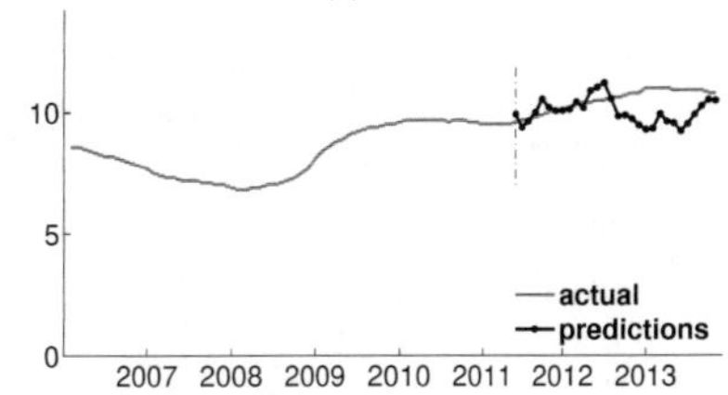


(b) Unemployment

Figure 1: Time series of ESI and unemployment together with BEN predictions (smoothed using a 3-point moving average).

alisation, where the font size is proportional to the derived weights by applying BEN, flipped terms denote negative weights and colours are determined by the frequency of use in the corpus (Fig. 2). Word clouds depict the top-60 positively and negatively weighted n-grams (120 in total) together with the top-30 outlets; bigrams are separated by '__'.

## 5 Discussion and Future Work

Our visualisations (Fig. 2) present various interesting insights into the news and socioeconomic features being explored, serving as a demonstration of the potential power of the proposed modelling. Firstly, we notice that in the word cloud, the size of a feature (BEN's weight) is not tightly connected with its colour (frequency in the corpus). Also, the word clouds suggest that mostly different terms and outlets are selected for the two indicators. For example, '*sky.it*' is predominant for ESI but not for unemployment, while the opposite is true for '*hedgefundsreview.com*'. Some of the words selected for ESI reflect economical issues, such as '*stimulus*' and '*spending*', whereas key politicians

(a) ESI

(b) Unemployment

Figure 2: Word clouds for words and outlets visualising the outputs of BEN.

like '*david__cameron*' and '*berlusconi*', are major participants in the word cloud for unemployment. In addition, the visualisations show a strong negative relationship between unemployment and the terms '*food*', '*russia*' and '*agriculture*', but no such relationship with respect to ESI. The disparity of these selections is evidence for our framework's capability to highlight features of lesser or greater importance to a given socioeconomic time series. The exact interpretation of the selected words and outlets is, perhaps, context-dependent and beyond the scope of this work.

In this paper, we presented a framework for performing a supervised analysis on news. An important factor for this process is that the bilinear nature of the learning function allows for a joint selection of important words and news outlets. Prediction performance is used as a reference point for determining whether the extracted outputs (i.e. the model's parameters) encapsulate relevant information regarding to the given indicator. Experiments were conducted on a set of EU-related news summaries and the supervising socioeconomic factors were the EU-wide ESI and unemployment. BEN outperformed the linear alternative (LEN), producing error rates below $8.8\%$.

The performance of our framework motivates several extensions to be explored in future work. Firstly, the incorporation of additional textual features may improve predictive capability and allow for richer interpretations of the term weights. For example, we could extend our term vocabulary using $n$-grams with $n > 2$, POS tags of words and entities (people, companies, places, etc.). Furthermore, multi-task learning approaches as well as models which incorporate the regularised learning of weights for different countries might give us further insights into the relationship between news, geographic location and socioeconomic indicators. Most importantly, we plan to gain a better understanding of the outputs by conducting a thorough analysis in collaboration with domain experts.

## Acknowledgements

VL acknowledges the support from the EPSRC IRC project EP/K031953/1. DPP, SS, DG and TC were supported by EU-FP7-ICT project n.287863 ("TrendMiner").

## References

R. Alexander Bentley, Alberto Acerbi, Paul Ormerod, and Vasileios Lampos. 2014. Books average previous decade of economic misery. *PLoS ONE*, 9(1).

Steven Bird, Ewan Klein, and Edward Loper. 2009. *Natural Language Processing with Python*. O'Reilly Media.

Johan Bollen and Huina Mao. 2011. Twitter mood as a stock market predictor. *IEEE Computer*, 44(10):91–94.

Munmun De Choudhury, Scott Counts, and Eric Horvitz. 2013. Social media as a measurement tool of depression in populations. In *Proceedings of ACM WebSci'13*, pages 47–56.

European Commision. 1997. *The joint harmonised EU programme of business and consumer surveys*. European economy: Reports and studies.

Ilias Flaounas, Marco Turchi, Omar Ali, Nick Fyson, Tijl De Bie, Nick Mosdell, Justin Lewis, and Nello Cristianini. 2010. The Structure of the EU Mediasphere. *PLoS ONE*, 5(12), 12.

Sarah Gelper and Christophe Croux. 2010. On the construction of the European Economic Sentiment Indicator. *Oxford Bulletin of Economics and Statistics*, 72(1):47–62.

Trevor Hastie, Robert Tibshirani, and Jerome Friedman. 2009. *The Elements of Statistical Learning: Data Mining, Inference, and Prediction*. Springer.

Arthur E. Hoerl and Robert W. Kennard. 1970. Ridge regression: biased estimation for nonorthogonal problems. *Technometrics*, 12:55–67.

Vasileios Lampos and Nello Cristianini. 2012. Nowcasting events from the Social Web with statistical learning. *ACM TIST*, 3(4):72:1–72:22.

Vasileios Lampos, Daniel Preoţiuc-Pietro, and Trevor Cohn. 2013. A user-centric model of voting intention from Social Media. In *Proceedings of ACL'13*, pages 993–1003.

Carolyn Lin, Michael B. Salwen, Bruce Garrison, and Paul D. Driscoll. 2005. Online news as a functional substitute for offline news. *Online news and the public*, pages 237–255.

Seungahn Nah and Deborah S. Chung. 2012. When citizens meet both professional and citizen journalists: Social trust, media credibility, and perceived journalistic roles among online community news readers. *Journalism*, 13(6):714–730.

Brendan O'Connor, Ramnath Balasubramanyan, Bryan R. Routledge, and Noah A. Smith. 2010. From tweets to polls: linking text sentiment to public opinion time series. In *Proceedings of AAAI ICWSM'10*, pages 122–129.

Michael J. Paul and Mark Dredze. 2011. You Are What You Tweet: Analyzing Twitter for Public Health. In *Proceedings of AAAI ICWSM'11*, pages 265–272.

Robert P. Schumaker and Hsinchun Chen. 2009. Textual analysis of stock market prediction using breaking financial news: the AZFin text system. *ACM TOIS*, 27(2):12:1–12:19.

H. Andrew Schwartz, Johannes C. Eichstaedt, Margaret L. Kern, Lukasz Dziurzynski, Stephanie M. Ramones, Megha Agrawal, Achal Shah, Michal Kosinski, David Stillwell, Martin E. P. Seligman, and Lyle H. Ungar. 2013. Personality, Gender, and Age in the Language of Social Media: The Open-Vocabulary Approach. *PLoS ONE*, 8(9).

Robert Tibshirani. 1994. Regression shrinkage and selection via the lasso. *JRSS: Series B*, 58:267–288.

Hui Zou and Trevor Hastie. 2005. Regularization and variable selection via the elastic net. *JRSS: Series B*, 67(2):301–320.

# Fact Checking: Task definition and dataset construction

**Andreas Vlachos**
Dept. of Computer Science
University College London
London, United Kingdom
a.vlachos@cs.ucl.ac.uk

**Sebastian Riedel**
Dept. of Computer Science
University College London
London, United Kingdom
s.riedel@ucl.ac.uk

## Abstract

In this paper we introduce the task of fact checking, i.e. the assessment of the truthfulness of a claim. The task is commonly performed manually by journalists verifying the claims made by public figures. Furthermore, ordinary citizens need to assess the truthfulness of the increasing volume of statements they consume. Thus, developing fact checking systems is likely to be of use to various members of society. We first define the task and detail the construction of a publicly available dataset using statements fact-checked by journalists available online. Then, we discuss baseline approaches for the task and the challenges that need to be addressed. Finally, we discuss how fact checking relates to mainstream natural language processing tasks and can stimulate further research.

## 1 Motivation

Fact checking is the task of assessing the truthfulness of claims made by public figures such as politicians, pundits, etc. It is commonly performed by journalists employed by news organisations in the process of news article creation. More recently, institutes and websites dedicated to this cause have emerged such as Full Fact[1] and PolitiFact[2] respectively. Figure 1 shows two examples of fact checked statements, together with the verdicts offered by the journalists.

Fact-checking is a time-consuming process. In assessing the first claim in Figure 1 a journalist would need to consult a variety of sources to find the average "full-time earnings" for criminal barristers. Fact checking websites commonly provide the detailed analysis (not shown in the figure) performed to support the verdict.

Automating the process of fact checking has recently been discussed in the context of computational journalism (Cohen et al., 2011; Flew et al., 2012). Inspired by the recent progress in natural language processing, databases and information retrieval, the vision is to provide journalists with tools that would allow them to perform this task automatically, or even render the articles "live" by updating them with most current data. This automation is further enabled by the increasing online availability of datasets, survey results, and reports in machine readable formats by various institutions, e.g. EUROSTAT releases detailed statistics for all European economies.[3]

Furthermore, ordinary citizens need to fact check the information provided to them. This need is intensified with the proliferation of social media such as Twitter, since the dissemination of news and information commonly circumvents the traditional news channels (Petrovic, 2013). In addition, the rise of citizen journalism (Goode, 2009) suggests that often citizens become the sources of information. Since the information provided by them is not edited or curated, automated fact checking would assist in avoiding the spreading false information.

In this paper we define the task of fact-checking. We then detail the construction of a dataset using fact-checked statements available online. Finally, we describe the challenges it poses and its relation to current research in natural language processing.

[1] http://fullfact.org
[2] http://politifact.com
[3] http://epp.eurostat.ec.europa.eu/portal/page/portal/eurostat/home



*Proceedings of the ACL 2014 Workshop on Language Technologies and Computational Social Science*, pages 18–22,
Baltimore, Maryland, USA, June 26, 2014. 

## 2 Task definition

We define fact-checking to be the assignment of a truth value to a claim made in a particular context. Thus it is natural to consider it as a binary classification task. However, it is often the case that the statements are not completely true or false. For example, the verdict for the third claim in Figure 1 is MostlyTrue because some of the sources dispute it, while in the fourth example the statistics can be manipulated to support or disprove the claim as desired. Therefore it is better to consider fact-checking as an ordinal classification task (Frank and Hall, 2001), thus allowing systems to capture the nuances of the task.

The verdict by itself, even if graded, needs to be supported by an analysis (e.g., what is the systems interpretation of the statement). However, given the difficulty of carving out exactly what the correct analysis for a statement might be, we restrict the task to be a prediction problem so that we can evaluate performance automatically.

Context can be crucial in fact-checking. For example, knowing that the fourth claim of Figure 1 is made by a UK politician is necessary in order to assess it using data about this country. Furthermore, time is also important since the various comparisons usually refer to time-frames anchored at the time a claim is made.

The task is rather challenging. While some claims such as the one about Crimea can be fact-checked by extracting relations from WikiPedia, the verdict often hinges on interpreting relatively fine points, e.g. the last claim refers to a particular definition of income. Journalists also check multiple sources in producing their verdicts, as in the case of the third claim. Interestingly, they also consider multiple interpretations of the data; e.g. in the last claim is assessed as HalfTrue since different but reasonable interpretations of the same data lead to different conclusions.

We consider all of the aspects mentioned (time, speaker, multiple sources and interpretations) as part of the task of fact checking. However, we want to restrict the task to statements that can be fact-checked objectively, which is not always true for the statements assessed by journalists. Therefore, we do not consider statements such as "New Labour promised social improvement but delivered a collapse in social mobility" to be part to the task since there are no universal definitions of "social improvement" and "social mobility".[4]

[4] http://blogs.channel4.com/factcheck/factcheck-social-mobility-collapsed/

**Claim** *(by Minister Shailesh Vara)*

"The average criminal bar barrister working full-time is earning some £84,000."

**Verdict:** False *(by Channel 4 Fact Check)*

The figures the Ministry of Justice have stressed this week seem decidedly dodgy. Even if you do want to use the figures, once you take away the many overheads self-employed advocates have to pay you are left with a middling sum of money.

**Claim** *(by U.S. Rep. Mike Rogers)*

"Crimea was part of Russia until 1954, when it was given to the Soviet Republic of the Ukraine."

**Verdict:** True *(by Politifact)*

Rogers said Crimea belonged to Russia until 1954, when Khrushchev gave the land to Ukraine, then a Soviet republic.

**Claim** *(by President Barack Obama)*

"For the first time in over a decade, business leaders around the world have declared that China is no longer the world's No. 1 place to invest; America is."

**Verdict:** MostlyTrue *(by Politifact)*

The president is accurate by citing one particular study, and that study did ask business leaders what they thought about investing in the United States. A broader look at other rankings doesn't make the United States seem like such a powerhouse, even if it does still best China in some lists.

**Claim** *(by Chancellor George Osborne)*

"Real household disposable income is rising."

**Verdict:** HalfTrue *(by Channel 4 Fact Check)*

RHDI did grow in latest period we know about (the second quarter of 2013), making Mr Osborne arguably right to say that it is rising as we speak. But over the last two quarters we know about, income was down 0.1 per cent. If you want to compare the latest four quarters of data with the previous four, there was a fall in household income, making the chancellor wrong. But if you compare the latest full year of results, 2012, with 2011, income is up and he's right again.

Figure 1: Fact-checked statements.

## 3 Dataset construction

In order to construct a dataset to develop and evaluate approaches to fact checking, we first surveyed popular fact checking websites. We decided to consider statements from two of them, the fact checking blog of Channel 4[5] and the Truth-O-Meter from PolitiFact.[6] Both websites have large archives of fact-checked statements (more than 1,000 statements each), they cover a wide range of prevalent issues of U.K. and U.S. public life, and they provide detailed verdicts with fine-grained labels such as MOSTLYFALSE and HALFTRUE.

We examined recent fact-checks from each website at the time of writing. For each statement, apart from the statement itself, we recorded the date it was made, the speaker, the label of the verdict and the URL. As the two websites use different labelling schemes, we aligned the labels of the verdicts to a five-point scale: TRUE, MOSTLYTRUE, HALFTRUE, MOSTLYFALSE and FALSE. The speakers included, apart from public figures, associations such as the American Beverage Association, activists, even viral FaceBook posts submitted by the public.

We then decided which of the statements should be considered for the task proposed. As discussed in the previous section we want to avoid statements that cannot be assessed objectively. Following this, we deemed unsuitable statements:

- assessing causal relations, e.g. whether a statistic should be attributed to a particular law
- concerning the future, e.g. speculations involving oil prices
- not concerning facts, e.g. whether a politician is supporting certain policies

For the statements that were considered suitable, we also collected the sources used by the journalists in the analysis provided for the verdict. Common sources include tables with statistics and reports from governments, think tanks and other organisations, available online. Automatic identification of the sources needed to fact check a statement is an important stage in the process, which is potentially useful in its own right in the context of assisting journalists in a semi-automated fact-checking approach Cohen et al. (2011). Sometimes the verdicts relied on data that were not available online such personal communications; statements whose verdict relied on such data were also deemed unsuitable for the task.

As mentioned earlier, the verdicts on the websites are accompanied by lengthy analyses. While such analyses could be useful annotation for intermediate stages of the task — e.g. we could use it as supervision to learn how to combine the information extracted from the various sources into a verdict — we noticed that the language used in them is indicative of the verdict.[7] Thus we decided not to include them in the dataset, as it would enable tackling part of the task as sentiment analysis. Out of the 221 fact-checked statements examined, we judged 106 as suitable. The dataset collected including our suitability judgements is publicly available[8] and we are working on extending it so that it can support the development and the automatic evaluation of fact checking approaches.

## 4 Baseline approaches

As discussed in Section 2, we consider fact checking as an ordinal classification task. Thus, in theory it would be possible to tackle it as a supervised classification task using algorithms that learn from statements annotated with the verdict labels. However this is unlikely to be successful, since statements such as the ones verified by journalists do not contain the world knowledge and the temporal and spatial context needed for this purpose.

A different approach would be to match statements to ones already fact-checked by journalists and return the label in a K-nearest neighbour fashion.[9] Thus the task is reduced to assessing the semantic similarity between statements, which was explored in a recent shared task (Agirre et al., 2013). An obvious shortcoming of this approach is that it cannot be applied to new claims that have not been fact-checked, thus it can only be used to detect repetitions and paraphrases of false claims.

A possible mechanism to extend the coverage of such an approach to novel statements is to assume that some large text collection is the source of all true statements. For example, Wikipedia is likely

16444

[5] `http://blogs.channel4.com/factcheck/`

[6] `http://www.politifact.com/truth-o-meter/statements/`

[7] E.g. part of the analysis of the first claim in Figure 1 reads: "the full-time figure has the handy effect of stripping out the very lowest earners and bumping up the average".

[8] `https://sites.google.com/site/andreasvlachos/resources`

[9] The Truth-Teller by Washington Post (`http://truthteller.washingtonpost.com/`) follows this approach.

to contain a statement that would match the second claim in Figure 1. However, it would still be unable to tackle the other claims mentioned, since they require calculations based on the data.

## 5 Discussion

The main drawback of the baseline approaches mentioned (aside from their potential coverage) is the lack of interpretability of their verdicts, also referred to as algorithmic accountability (Diakopoulos, 2014). While it is possible for a natural language processing expert to inspect aspects of the prediction such as feature weights, this tends to become harder as the approaches become more sophisticated. Ultimately, the user of a fact checking system would trust a verdict only if it is accompanied by an analysis similar to the one provided by the journalists. This desideratum is present in other tasks such as the recently proposed science test question answering (Clark et al., 2013).

Cohen et al. (2011) propose that fact checking is about asking the right questions. These questions might be database queries, requests for information to be extracted from textual resources, etc. For example, in checking the last claim in Figure 1 a critical reader would like to know what are the possible interpretations of "real household disposable income" and what the calculations might be for other reasonable time spans.

The manual fact checking process suggests an approach that is more likely to give an interpretable analysis and would decompose the task into the following stages:

1. extract statements to be fact-checked
2. construct appropriate questions
3. obtain the answers from relevant sources
4. reach a verdict using these answers

The stages of this architecture can be mapped to tasks well-explored in the natural language processing community. Statement extraction could be tackled as a sentence classification problem, following approaches similar to those proposed for speculation detection (Farkas et al., 2010) and veridicality assessment (de Marneffe et al., 2012). Furthermore, obtaining answers to questions from databases is a task typically addressed in the context of semantic parsing research, while obtaining such answers from textual sources is usually considered in the context of information extraction. Finally, the compilation of the answers into a verdict could be considered as a form of logic-based textual entailment (Bos and Markert, 2005).

However, the fact-checking stages described include a novel task, namely question construction for a given statement. This task is likely to rely on semantic parsing of the statement followed by restructuring of the logical form generated. Since question construction is a rather uncommon task, it is likely to require human supervision, which could possibly be obtained via crowdsourcing. Furthermore, the open-domain nature of fact checking places greater demands on the established tasks of information extraction and semantic parsing. Thus, fact-checking is likely to stimulate research in these tasks on methods that do not require domain-specific supervision (Riedel et al., 2013) and are able to adapt to new information requests (Kwiatkowski et al., 2013).

Fact-checking is related to the tasks of textual entailment (Dagan et al., 2006) and machine comprehension (Richardson et al., 2013), with the difference that the text which should be used to predict the entailment of the hypothesis or the correct answer respectively is not provided in the input. Instead, systems need to locate the sources needed to predict the verdict label as part of the task. Furthermore, by defining the task in the context of real-world journalism we are able to obtain labeled statements at no annotation cost, apart from the assessment of their suitability for the task.

## 6 Conclusions

In this paper we introduced the task of fact checking and detailed the construction of a dataset using statements fact-checked by journalists available online. In addition, we discussed baseline approaches that could be applied to perform the task and the challenges that need to be addressed.

Apart from being a challenging testbed to stimulate progress in natural language processing, research in fact checking is likely to inhibit the intentional or unintentional dissemination of false information. Even an approach that would return the sources related to a statement could be very helpful to journalists as well as other critical readers in a semi-automated fact checking approach.

## Acknowledgments

The authors would like to thank the members of the Machine Reading lab for useful discussions and their help in compiling the dataset.

## References


Eneko Agirre, Daniel Cer, Mona Diab, Aitor Gonzalez-Agirre, and Weiwei Guo. 2013. *sem 2013 shared task: Semantic textual similarity. In *Proceedings of the Second Joint Conference on Lexical and Computational Semantics and the Shared Task: Semantic Textual Similarity*, pages 32–43, Atlanta, GA.

Johan Bos and Katja Markert. 2005. Recognising textual entailment with logical inference. In *Proceedings of the 2005 Conference on Empirical Methods in Natural Language Processing (EMNLP 2005)*, pages 628–635.

Peter Clark, Philip Harrison, and Niranjan Balasubramanian. 2013. A study of the knowledge base requirements for passing an elementary science test. In *Proceedings of the 2013 Workshop on Automated Knowledge Base Construction*, pages 37–42.

Sarah Cohen, Chengkai Li, Jun Yang, and Cong Yu. 2011. Computational journalism: A call to arms to database researchers. In *Proceedings of the Conference on Innovative Data Systems Research*, volume 2011, pages 148–151.

Ido Dagan, Oren Glickman, and Bernardo Magnini. 2006. The pascal recognising textual entailment challenge. In *Proceedings of the First International Conference on Machine Learning Challenges: Evaluating Predictive Uncertainty Visual Object Classification, and Recognizing Textual Entailment*, pages 177–190.

Marie-Catherine de Marneffe, Christopher D. Manning, and Christopher Potts. 2012. Did it happen? the pragmatic complexity of veridicality assessment. *Computational Linguistics*, 38(2):301–333, June.

Nick Diakopoulos. 2014. Algorithmic accountability reporting: On the investigation of black boxes. Technical report, Tow Center for Digital Journalism.

Richard Farkas, Veronika Vincze, Gyorgy Mora, Janos Csirik, and Gyorgy Szarvas. 2010. The CoNLL 2010 Shared Task: Learning to Detect Hedges and their Scope in Natural Language Text. In *Proceedings of the CoNLL 2010 Shared Task*.

Terry Flew, Anna Daniel, and Christina L. Spurgeon. 2012. The promise of computational journalism. In *Proceedings of the Australian and New Zealand Communication Association Conference*, pages 1–19.

Eibe Frank and Mark Hall. 2001. A simple approach to ordinal classification. In *Proceedings of the 12th European Conference on Machine Learning*, pages 145–156.

Luke Goode. 2009. Social news, citizen journalism and democracy. *New Media & Society*, 11(8):1287–1305.

Tom Kwiatkowski, Eunsol Choi, Yoav Artzi, and Luke Zettlemoyer. 2013. Scaling semantic parsers with on-the-fly ontology matching. In *Proceedings of the 2013 Conference on Empirical Methods in Natural Language Processing*, pages 1545–1556, Seattle, WA.

Sasa Petrovic. 2013. *Real-time event detection in massive streams*. Ph.D. thesis, School of Informatics, University of Edinburgh.

Matthew Richardson, Christopher J.C. Burges, and Erin Renshaw. 2013. MCTest: A challenge dataset for the open-domain machine comprehension of text. In *Proceedings of the 2013 Conference on Empirical Methods in Natural Language Processing*, pages 193–203, Seattle, WA.

Sebastian Riedel, Limin Yao, Benjamin M. Marlin, and Andrew McCallum. 2013. Relation extraction with matrix factorization and universal schemas. In *Proceedings of the 2013 Conference of the North American Chapter of the Association for Computational Linguistics: Human Language Technologies*, Atlanta, GA.

# Finding Eyewitness Tweets During Crises

**Fred Morstatter[1], Nichola Lubold[1], Heather Pon-Barry[1], Jürgen Pfeffer[2], and Huan Liu[1]**
[1]Arizona State University, Tempe, Arizona, USA
[2]Carnegie Mellon University, Pittsburgh, Pennsylvania, USA
{fred.morstatter, nlubold, ponbarry, huan.liu}@asu.edu, jpfeffer@cs.cmu.edu

## Abstract

Disaster response agencies incorporate social media as a source of fast-breaking information to understand the needs of people affected by the many crises that occur around the world. These agencies look for tweets from within the region affected by the crisis to get the latest updates on the status of the affected region. However only 1% of all tweets are "geotagged" with explicit location information. In this work we seek to identify non-geotagged tweets that originate from within the crisis region. Towards this, we address three questions: (1) is there a difference between the language of tweets originating within a crisis region, (2) what linguistic patterns differentiate within-region and outside-region tweets, and (3) can we automatically identify those originating within the crisis region in real-time?

## 1 Introduction

Due to Twitter's massive popularity, it has become a tool used by first responders—those who provide first-hand aid in times of crisis—to understand crisis situations and identify the people in the most dire need of assistance (United Nations, 2012). To do this, first responders can survey "geotagged" tweets: those where the user has supplied a geographic location. The advantage of geotagged tweets is that first responders know whether a person is tweeting from within the affected region or is tweeting from afar. Tweets from within this region are more likely to contain emerging topics (Kumar et al., 2013) and tactical, actionable, information that contribute to situational awareness (Verma et al., 2011).

A major limitation of surveying geotagged tweets is that only 1% of all tweets are geotagged (Morstatter et al., 2013). This leaves the first responders unable to tap into the vast majority of the tweets they collect. This limitation leads to the question driving this work: can we discover whether a tweet originates from within a crisis region using *only the language used of the tweet*?

We focus on the language of a tweet as the defining factor of location for three major reasons: (1) the language of Twitter users is dependent on their location (Cheng et al., 2010), (2) the text is readily available in every tweet, and (3) the text allows for real-time analysis. Due to the short time window presented by most crises, first responders need to be able to locate users quickly.

Towards this goal, we examine tweets from two recent crises: the Boston Marathon bombing and Hurricane Sandy. We show that linguistic differences exist between tweets authored inside and outside the affected regions. By analyzing the text of individual tweets we can predict whether the tweet originates from within the crisis region, in real-time. To better understand the characteristics of crisis-time language on Twitter, we conclude with a discussion of the linguistic features that our models find most discriminative.

## 2 Language Differences in Crises

In order for a language-based approach to be able to distinguish tweets inside of the crisis region, the language used by those in the region during crisis has to be different from those outside. In this section, we verify that there are both regional and temporal differences in the language tweeted. To start, we introduce the data sets we use throughout the rest of this paper. We then measure the difference in language, finding that language changes temporally and regionally at the time of the crisis.

### 2.1 Twitter Crisis Datasets

The Twitter data used in our experiments comes from two crises: the Boston Marathon bombing and Hurricane Sandy. Both events provoked a significant Twitter response from within and beyond



*Proceedings of the ACL 2014 Workshop on Language Technologies and Computational Social Science*, pages 23–27,
Baltimore, Maryland, USA, June 26, 2014. 

Table 1: Properties of the Twitter crisis datasets.

| Property | Boston | Sandy |
|---|---|---|
| Crisis Start | 15 Apr 14:48 | 29 Oct 20:00 |
| Crisis End | 16 Apr 00:00 | 30 Oct 01:00 |
| Epicenter | 42.35, −71.08 | 40.75, −73.99 |
| Radius | 19 km | 20 km |
| $\|\mathbf{IR}\|$ | 11,601 | 5,017 |
| $\|\mathbf{OR}\|$ | 541,581 | 195,957 |
| $\|\mathbf{PC\text{-}IR}\|$ | 14,052 | N/A |
| $\|\mathbf{PC\text{-}OR}\|$ | 228,766 | N/A |

the affected regions.

The **Boston Marathon Bombing** occurred at the finish line of the Boston Marathon on April 15th, 2013 at 14:48 Eastern. We collected geotagged tweets from the continental United States from 2013-04-09 00:00 to 2013-04-22 00:00 utilizing Twitter's Filter API.

**Hurricane Sandy** was a "superstorm" that ravaged the Eastern United States in October, 2012. Utilizing Twitter's Filter API, we collected tweets based on several keywords pertaining to the storm. Filtering by keywords, this dataset contains both geotagged and non-geotagged data beginning from the day the storm made landfall (2012-10-29) to several days after (2012-11-02).

### 2.2 Data Partitioning

For the Boston Bombing and Hurricane Sandy datasets, we partitioned the tweets published *during the crisis time* into two distinct parts based on location: (1) inside the crisis region (**IR**), and (2) outside the crisis region (**OR**).

For the Boston Bombing dataset, we are able to extract two additional groups: (1) pre-crisis tweets (posted before the time of the crisis) from inside the crisis region (**PC-IR**) and (2) pre-crisis tweets from outside the crisis region (**PC-OR**). We take a time-based sample from 10:00–14:48 Eastern on April 15th, 2013 to obtain **PC-IR** and **PC-OR**. Because the bombing was an abrupt event with no warning, we choose a time period immediately preceding its onset. The number of tweets in each dataset partition is shown in Table 1.

### 2.3 Pre-Crisis vs. During-Crisis Language

For the Boston dataset, we compare the words used hour by hour between 10:00–19:00 on April 15th. For each pair of hours, we compute the Jensen-Shannon (J-S) divergence (Lin, 1991) of the probability distributions of the words used

(a) Temporal language differences. (b) Geographic language differences: tranquil time. (c) Geographic language differences: crisis time.

Figure 1: Temporal and geographic differences of language (calculated using Jensen-Shannon divergence); darker shades represent greater difference. To illustrate geographic differences, we compare Boston with three other major U.S. cities.

within those hours. Figure 1(a) shows these J-S divergence values. We see an abrupt change in language in the hours before the bombing (10:00–14:00) and those after the bombing (15:00–19:00). We also note that the tranquil hours are relatively stable. This suggests that language models trained on tweets from tranquil time are less informative for modeling crisis-time langauge.

### 2.4 IR vs. OR Language

We verify that the tweets authored inside of the crisis use different words from those outside the region. We compare the difference in Boston (**B**) to three other major U.S. cities: Chicago (**C**), Los Angeles (**L**), and Miami (**M**). To obtain a baseline, we compare the cities during tranquil times using **PC-IR** and **PC-OR** datasets. The results are shown in Figure 1. The tranquil time comparison, shown in Figure 1(b), displays a low divergence between all pairs of cities. In contrast, Figure 1(c) shows a wider divergence between the same cities, with Boston displaying the greatest divergence.

## 3 Linguistic Features

As Twitter is a conversational, real-time, microblogging site, the structure of tweets offers many opportunities for extracting different types of features that represent the different linguistic properties of informal text. Our approach is to compare the utility, in classifying tweets as **IR** or **OR**, of several linguistic features. We preprocess the tweets by extracting tokens using the CMU Twitter NLP tokenizer (Owoputi et al., 2013).

**Unigrams** and **Bigrams** We extract the raw frequency counts of the word unigrams and bigrams.

**POS Tags** We extract part-of-speech tags for each word in the tweet using the CMU Twitter NLP POS tagger (Owoputi et al., 2013). We consider CMU ARK POS tags, developed specifically for the dynamic and informal nature of tweets, as well as Penn Treebank (PTB) style POS tags. The ARK POS tags are coarser than the PTB tags and can identify Twitter-specific entities in the data like hashtags. By comparing both tag sets, we can measure the effectiveness of both the fine-grained versus coarse-grained tag sets.

**Shallow Parsing** In addition to the POS tags, we extract shallow parsing tags along with the headword associated with the tag using the tool provided by Ritter et al. (2011). For example, in the noun phrase "the movie" we would extract the headword "movie" and represent it as $[...\text{movie}...]_{NP}$. The underlying motivation is that this class may give more insight into the syntactic differences of **IR** tweets versus **OR** tweets.

**Crisis-Sensitive (CS) Features** We create a mixed-class of "crisis sensitive" features composed of *word-based*, *part of speech*, and *syntactic constituent* attributes. These are based on our analysis of the Boston Marathon data set. We later apply these features to the Hurricane Sandy data set to validate whether the features are generalizable across crises and discuss this in the results.

- We extract **"in" prepositional phrases** of the form $[\text{in} ... /\text{N}]_{PP}$. For example, "in Boston." The motivation is this use of "in," such as with a location or a nonspecific time, may be indicative of crisis language.
- We extract verbs in relationship to the **existential *there***. As the existential *there* is usually the grammatical subject and describes an abstraction, it may be indicative of situational awareness messages within the disaster region.
- **Part-of-Speech tag sequences** that are frequent in IR tweets (from our development set) are given special consideration. We find sequences which are used more widely during the time of this disaster. Some of the ARK tag sequences include: ⟨N R⟩, ⟨L A⟩, ⟨N P⟩, ⟨P D N⟩, ⟨L A !⟩, ⟨A N P⟩.

# 4 Experiments

Here, we assess the effectiveness of our linguistic features at the task of identifying tweets originating from within the crisis region. To do this we use a Naïve Bayes classifier configured with an individual set of feature classes. Each of our features are represented as raw frequency counts of the number of times they occur within the tweet. The output is a prediction of whether the tweet is inside region (**IR**) or outside region (**OR**). We identify the features that can differentiate the two classes of users, and we show that this process can indeed be automated.

Table 2: Top Feature Combinations: Unigrams (Uni), Bigrams (Bi) and Crisis-Sensitive (CS) combinations have the best results.

| Top Feature Combos | Prec. | Recall | F1 |
|---|---|---|---|
| | **Boston Bombing** | | |
| Uni + Bi | 0.853 | 0.805 | 0.828 |
| Uni + Bi + Shallow Parse | 0.892 | 0.771 | 0.828 |
| **Uni + Bi + CS** | 0.857 | 0.806 | **0.831** |
| All Features | 0.897 | 0.742 | 0.812 |
| | **Hurricane Sandy** | | |
| Uni + Bi | 0.942 | 0.820 | 0.877 |
| Uni + Bi + Shallow Parse + CS | 0.956 | 0.803 | 0.873 |
| **Uni + Bi + CS** | 0.947 | 0.826 | **0.882** |
| All Features | 0.960 | 0.786 | 0.864 |

## 4.1 Experiment Procedure

We ensure a 50/50 split of **IR** and **OR** instances by sampling the **OR** dataset. Using the classifier described above, we perform $3 \times 5$-fold cross validation on the data. Because of the 50/50 split, a "select-all" baseline that labels all tweets as **IR** will have an accuracy of 50%, a precision of 50%, and a recall of 100%. All precision and recall values are from the perspective of the **IR** class.

## 4.2 Feature Class Analysis

We compare all possible combinations of individual feature classes and we report precision, recall, and F1-scores for the best combinations in Table 2.

In both crises all of the top performing feature combinations contain both bigram and unigram feature classes. However, our top performing feature combinations demonstrate that bigrams in combination with unigrams have added utility. We also see that the crisis-sensitive features are present in the top performing combinations for both data sets. The CS feature class was derived from Boston Bombing data, so its presence in the top groups from Hurricane Sandy is an indication that these features are general, and may be useful for finding users in these and future crises.

## 4.3 Most Informative Linguistic Features

To see which individual features within the classes give the best information, we make a modification to the experiment setup described in Section 4.1: we replace the Naïve Bayes classifier with a Logistic Regression classifier to utilize the coefficients it learns as a metric for feature importance. We report the top three features of each class label from each feature set in Table 3.

The individual unigram and bigram features with the most weight have a clear semantic rela-

Table 3: Top 3 features indicative of each class within each feature set for both crises.

| Feature Set (Class) | Boston Marathon Bombing | Hurricane Sandy |
|---|---|---|
| Unigram (**IR**) | #prayforboston, boston, explosion | @kiirkobangz, upset, staying |
| Unigram (**OR**) | money, weather, gone | #tomyfuturechildren, #tomyfutureson, bye |
| Bigram (**IR**) | ⟨in boston⟩, ⟨the marathon⟩, ⟨i'm safe⟩ | ⟨railroad :⟩, ⟨evacuation zone⟩, ⟨storm warning⟩ |
| Bigram (**OR**) | ⟨i'm at⟩, ⟨s/o to⟩, ⟨, fl⟩ | ⟨you will⟩, ⟨: i've⟩, ⟨hurricane ,⟩ |
| ARK POS (**IR**) | ⟨P $ ^⟩, ⟨L !⟩, ⟨! R P⟩ | ⟨P #⟩, ⟨~ ^ A⟩, ⟨@ @ #⟩ |
| ARK POS (**OR**) | ⟨O #⟩, ⟨! N O⟩, ⟨L P R⟩ | ⟨P V $⟩, ⟨A ^ ^⟩, ⟨N L A⟩ |
| PTB POS (**IR**) | ⟨CD NN JJ⟩, ⟨CD VBD⟩, ⟨JJS NN TO⟩ | ⟨USR DT JJS⟩, ⟨VB TO RB⟩, ⟨IN RB JJ⟩ |
| PTB POS (**OR**) | ⟨NNP -RRB-⟩, ⟨. JJ JJ⟩, ⟨JJ NN CD⟩ | ⟨NNS IN NNS⟩, ⟨PRP JJ PRP⟩, ⟨JJ NNP NNP⟩ |
| Shallow Parse (**IR**) | [...explosion...]$_{NP}$, [...marathon...]$_{NP}$, [...bombs...]$_{NP}$ | [...bomb...]$_{NP}$, [...waz...]$_{VP}$, [...evacuation...]$_{NP}$ |
| Shallow Parse (**OR**) | [...school...]$_{NP}$, [...song...]$_{NP}$, [...breakfast...]$_{NP}$ | [...school...]$_{NP}$, [...head...]$_{NP}$, [...wit...]$_{PP}$ |
| CS (**IR**) | [in boston/N]$_{PP}$, [for boston/N]$_{PP}$, ⟨i'm/L safe/A⟩ | ⟨while/P a/D hurricane/N⟩, ⟨of/P my/D house/N⟩, [in http://t.co/UxkKJLoX/N]$_{PP}$ |
| CS (**OR**) | ⟨to/P the/D beach/N⟩, [at la/N]$_{PP}$, [in love/N]$_{PP}$ | [like water/N]$_{PP}$, ⟨shutdowns/N on/P⟩, ⟨prayer/N for/P⟩ |

tionship to the crisis. Comparing the two crises, the top features for Hurricane Sandy are more concerned with user-user communication. For example, the heavily-weighted ARK POS trigram ⟨@ @ #⟩ is highly indicative of users spreading information between each other. One explanation is that the concern with communication could be a result of the warning that came from the storm. The bigram ⟨`hurricane ,`⟩ is the 3rd most indicative of a tweet originating from *outside* the region. This is likely because the word occurs in the general discussion outside of the crisis region.

## 5 Related Work

**Geolocation**: Eisenstein et al. (2010) first looked at the problem of using latent variables to explain the distribution of text in tweets. This problem was revisited from the perspective of geodesic grids in Wing and Baldridge (2011) and further improved by flexible adaptive grids (Roller et al., 2012). Cheng et al. (2010) employed an approach that looks at a user's tweets and estimates the user's location based on words with a local geographical scope. Han et al. (2013) combines tweet text with metadata to predict a user's location.

**Mass Emergencies**: De Longueville et al. (2009) study Twitter's use as a sensor for crisis information by studying the geographical properties of users' tweets. In Castillo et al. (2011), the authors analyze the text and social network of tweets to classify their newsworthiness. Kumar et al. (2013) use geotagged tweets to find emerging topics in crisis data. Investigating linguistic features, Verma et al. (2011) show the efficacy of language features at finding crisis-time tweets that contain tactical, actionable information, contributing to *situational awareness*. Using a larger dataset, we automatically discover linguistic features that can help with situational awareness.

## 6 Conclusion and Future Work

This paper addresses the challenge of finding tweets that originate from a crisis region using only the language of each tweet. We find that the tweets authored from within the crisis region do differ, from both tweets published during tranquil time periods and from tweets published from other geographic regions. We compare the utility of several linguistic feature classes that may help to distinguish the two classes and build a classifier based on these features to automate the process of identifying the **IR** tweets. We find that our classifier performs well and that this approach is suitable for attacking this problem.

Future work includes incorporating the wealth of tweets preceding the disaster for better predictions. Preliminary tests have shown positive results; for example we found early, non-geotagged reports of flooding in the Hoboken train tunnels during Hurricane Sandy[1]. Future work may also consider additional features, such as sentiment.

## Acknowledgments

This work is sponsored in part by the Office of Naval Research, grants N000141010091 and N000141110527, and the Ira A. Fulton Schools of Engineering, through fellowships to F. Morstatter and N. Lubold. We thank Alan Ritter and the ARK research group at CMU for sharing their tools.

[1]An extended version of this paper is available at: http://www.public.asu.edu/~fmorstat/paperpdfs/lang_loc.pdf.

## References


Carlos Castillo, Marcelo Mendoza, and Barbara Poblete. 2011. Information Credibility on Twitter. In *Proceedings of the 20th International Conference on World Wide Web*, pages 675–684. ACM.

Zhiyuan Cheng, James Caverlee, and Kyumin Lee. 2010. You Are Where You Tweet: A Content-Based Approach to Geo-locating Twitter Users. In *Proceedings of the 19th ACM International Conference on Information and Knowledge Management*, pages 759–768. ACM.

Bertrand De Longueville, Robin S Smith, and Gianluca Luraschi. 2009. "OMG, from here, I can see the flames!": a use case of mining Location Based Social Networks to acquire spatio-temporal data on forest fires. In *Proceedings of the 2009 International Workshop on Location Based Social Networks*, pages 73–80. ACM.

Jacob Eisenstein, Brendan O'Connor, Noah A Smith, and Eric P Xing. 2010. A Latent Variable Model for Geographic Lexical Variation. In *Proceedings of the 2010 Conference on Empirical Methods in Natural Language Processing*, pages 1277–1287. Association for Computational Linguistics.

Bo Han, Paul Cook, and Timothy Baldwin. 2013. A Stacking-based Approach to Twitter User Geolocation Prediction. In *Proceedings of the 51st Annual Meeting of the Association for Computational Linguistics (ACL 2013): System Demonstrations*, pages 7–12.

Shamanth Kumar, Fred Morstatter, Reza Zafarani, and Huan Liu. 2013. Whom Should I Follow?: Identifying Relevant Users During Crises. In *Proceedings of the 24th ACM Conference on Hypertext and Social Media*, HT '13, pages 139–147, New York, NY, USA. ACM.

Jianhua Lin. 1991. Divergence measures based on the shannon entropy. *IEEE Transactions on Information Theory*, 37(1):145–151.

Fred Morstatter, Jürgen Pfeffer, Huan Liu, and Kathleen M Carley. 2013. Is the Sample Good Enough? Comparing Data from Twitter's Streaming API with Twitter's Firehose. *Proceedings of The International Conference on Weblogs and Social Media.*

Olutobi Owoputi, Brendan O'Connor, Chris Dyer, Kevin Gimpel, Nathan Schneider, and Noah A Smith. 2013. Improved Part-of-Speech Tagging for Online Conversational Text with Word Clusters. In *Proceedings of NAACL-HLT*, pages 380–390.

Alan Ritter, Sam Clark, Mausam, and Oren Etzioni. 2011. Named entity recognition in tweets: An experimental study. In *EMNLP*.

Stephen Roller, Michael Speriosu, Sarat Rallapalli, Benjamin Wing, and Jason Baldridge. 2012. Supervised Text-Based Geolocation using Language Models on an Adaptive Grid. In *Proceedings of the 2012 Joint Conference on Empirical Methods in Natural Language Processing and Computational Natural Language Learning*, pages 1500–1510. Association for Computational Linguistics.

United Nations. 2012. *Humanitarianism in the Network Age*. United Nations Office for the Coordination of Humanitarian Affairs.

Sudha Verma, Sarah Vieweg, William J Corvey, Leysia Palen, James H Martin, Martha Palmer, Aaron Schram, and Kenneth Mark Anderson. 2011. Natural Language Processing to the Rescue? Extracting "Situational Awareness" Tweets During Mass Emergency. In *ICWSM*.

Benjamin Wing and Jason Baldridge. 2011. Simple Supervised Document Geolocation with Geodesic Grids. In *Proceedings of the 49th Annual Meeting of the Association for Computational Linguistics (ACL 2011)*, pages 955–964.

# Inducing Information Structures for Data-driven Text Analysis

**Andrew Salway**
Uni Research Computing
N-5008 Bergen
Norway
andrew.salway@uni.no

**Samia Touileb**
University of Bergen
N-5020 Bergen
Norway
samia.touileb@gmail.com

**Endre Tvinnereim**
Uni Research Rokkansenteret
N-5015 Bergen
Norway
endre.tvinnereim@uni.no

**Abstract**

We report ongoing work that is aiming to develop a data-driven approach to text analysis for computational social science. The novel feature is the use of a grammar induction algorithm to identify salient information structures from an unannotated text corpus. The structures provide richer representations of text content than keywords, by capturing patterning related to what is written about key terms. Here we show how information structures were induced from texts that record political negotiations, and how the structures were used in analyzing relations between countries and negotiation positions.

## 1 Introduction

There is a widespread need for automated text analysis to be integrated into research methods for computational social science (e.g. Grimmer and Stewart, 2013). In order to analyze highly diverse content, techniques tend to treat texts as bags of words, e.g. for search, to summarize content with word clouds, and to model topics. Such techniques capture the general "aboutness" of texts, but they do little to elucidate the actual statements that are made about key concepts. Conversely, structured representations of statements can be generated, up to a point, by information extraction systems but these are costly to port to new languages and domains.

Thus, we are motivated to develop a portable technique that can generate richer representations of text content than keywords. Our idea is to adapt and apply a grammar induction algorithm to identify salient information structures in the surface form of texts. It seems to us that, to the extent that there is patterning, information structures may be induced from an unannotated text corpus with little or no need for language-specific and domain-specific resources. Unlike approaches under the rubrics of unsupervised and open information extraction (e.g. Riloff, 1996; Sekine, 2006; Etzioni et al., 2008), we avoid the use of parsers, part-of-speech taggers, and pre-specified entities for which relations are sought.

The approach that we envisage fits with the ethos of exploratory "data-driven" research. Rather than approaching a corpus with a hypothesis and an a priori coding scheme, a researcher is given an overview of the content in terms of computationally tractable information structures that were induced from the corpus. Such structures map to surface forms in text and can hence be used directly in quantitative analyses for further exploration and to test hypotheses, once they have been interpreted as interesting by a researcher. Working in this way will avoid the expense and bottleneck of manual coding, and reduce the potential for biases.

In the following we motivate our use of the ADIOS algorithm for grammar induction (2.1), and introduce the Earth Negotiations Bulletin (2.2). Section 3 describes our method and discusses the information structures identified in ENB texts. Section 4 takes some preliminary steps in using these information structures to identify dyads of (dis-) agreement and to extract markers of quantifiable negotiation positions. In closing, Section 5 offers some tentative conclusions and ideas for future work.

## 2 Background

### 2.1 Grammar induction for text mining

Harris (1954; 1988) demonstrated how linguistic units and structures can be identified manually through a distributional analysis of partially aligned sentential contexts. We are struck by Harris' insight that the linguistic structures derived from a distributional analysis may reflect



*Proceedings of the ACL 2014 Workshop on Language Technologies and Computational Social Science*, pages 28–32,
Baltimore, Maryland, USA, June 26, 2014. 

domain-specific information structures, especially in the "sublanguages" of specialist domains (Harris, 1988). Whilst the textual material typically analyzed by social scientists may not be as restricted in content and style as that analyzed by Harris, our work proceeds on the assumption that, at least in some domains, it is restricted enough such that there is sufficient patterning for an inductive approach.

Harris' ideas about distributional analysis have become a cornerstone for some of the work in the field of automated grammatical inference, where researchers attempt to induce grammatical structures from raw text. In this field the emphasis is on generating complete grammatical descriptions for text corpora in order to understand the processes of language learning; see D'Ulizia et al. (2011) for a review.

For example, the unsupervised ADIOS algorithm (Solan et al., 2005) recursively induces hierarchically structured patterns from sequential data, e.g. sequences of words in sentences of unannotated text, using statistical information in the sequential data. Patterns may include equivalence classes comprising items that share similar distributional properties, where items may be words or other patterns. As a toy example of a pattern, take '(the (woman|man) went to the (house|shop|pub))', with equivalence classes '(woman|man)' and '(house|shop|pub)'.

### 2.2 The Earth Negotiations Bulletin

Within political science, text corpora provide a valuable resource for the analysis of political struggle and structures. For international climate negotiations, the Earth Negotiation Bulletin (ENB) constitutes an online record of the positions and proposals of different countries, their agreements and disagreements, and changes over time. As such it can provide insights into, e.g., how institutional structures and bargaining strategies affect policy outcomes. Since 1995, every day of formal climate negotiations under the UN Framework Convention on Climate Change (UN FCCC) and the Kyoto Protocol has been summarized in a separate 2-4 page issue of the ENB[1]. The ENB seeks to cover the major topics of discussion and which negotiators (referred to by country name) said what. The publication is used by scholars to address research questions such as whether countries with more extreme positions have more or less success (Weiler, 2012) and whether democracies and autocracies (Bailer, 2012) or developed and developing countries (Castro et al., 2014) behave differently in negotiations. From our perspective, the ENB's restricted content and style makes it appropriate to test our inductive approach.

## 3 Inducing Information Structures

We are investigating how the ADIOS algorithm (Solan et al., 2005) can be adapted and applied for mining the content of unannotated corpora; cf. Salway and Touileb (2014). Our objective of identifying salient information structures, rather than generating a complete grammatical description, leads us to modify the learning regime of ADIOS. Firstly, we modify the way in which text is presented to ADIOS by presenting sentences containing terms of interest (for the ENB texts these were country names), rather than processing all sentences: we expect more relevant patterning in these sentences, and think the patterning will be more explicit if not diluted by the rest of the corpus. Secondly, as described in more detail below, we focus the algorithm on frequent structures through an iterative process of selection and substitution.

### 3.1 Method

Our data set comprised all texts from the ENB volume 12, numbers 1-594, which cover the period 1995-2013. Preprocessing involved removing boilerplate text, sentence segmentation, and making all text lowercase. Then, all sentences mentioning one or more countries were selected. Every mention of a country, or a list of countries, was replaced with the token 'COUNTRY': this serves to make patterning around mentions of countries more explicit. A list of country names was the only domain- and language-specific resource required for the processing described below.

The resulting file of 32,288 sentences was processed by an implementation of the ADIOS algorithm, in which we modified the original learning regime to bias it towards frequent structures. After one execution of ADIOS we selected the five most frequent patterns (and any patterns contained within them) and replaced all instances of them in the input file with a unique identifier for each pattern: as with the 'COUNTRY' token, we believe that this serves to make relevant patterning more explicit. We executed ADIOS and selected and substituted frequent patterns nine more times.

[1] http://www.iisd.ca/linkages/vol12/

### 3.2 Results

In this way 53 patterns were identified, some of which are shown in Table 1 (patterns 1-7). Here patterns and equivalence classes are bracketed and nested. The sequential items in a pattern are separated by whitespace and the alternative items in an equivalence class are separated by '|'. 'COUNTRY' stands for a mention of a country, or a list of countries. In some cases we have manually merged and simplified patterns for clarity, but the structuring that they describe was all induced automatically.

Pattern 1 captures a simple relation between countries that appears frequently in sentences like 'China supported by Saudi Arabia said…'. It could thus be used as a simple template for extracting data about how countries align with one another (see section 4.1). Patterns 2-4 represent a multitude of ways in which a country's stated positions on issues can be reported. These patterns do not describe the issues, but could be used as cues to locate text fragments that do, e.g. by taking the text that follows 'COUNTRY said|noted|recommended|(etc.)…' (see section 4.2). Patterns 5 and 6 appear to have captured a wide variety of verbs and noun phrases respectively. Presumably these verbs relate to things that countries say that they will do, or that they think should be done. The noun phrases appear to raise topics for discussion; consider how pattern 6 appears as part of 7. There were other patterns that did not contain any equivalence classes: these often captured domain terminology, e.g. '(developing countries)', '(commitment period)'.

Patterns 1-6 all have a relatively shallow structure. In order to induce further structure we made new input files, based on what we saw in the initial patterns. We chose the most frequent 'speech acts' from patterns 2-4, and for each one made a separate file containing only sentences that contained 'COUNTRY SPEECH_ACT', e.g. one file that contained all the sentences matching 'COUNTRY expressed'. Each speech act file was processed with 10 iterations of selection and substitution (cf. section 3.1). The resulting patterns, including 8-10 in Table 1, do indeed have richer structures and show in a more nuanced way how countries' positions are reported in the ENB texts.

These results are encouraging for the idea of inducing information structures from an unannotated text corpus. The examples shown in Table 1 would not surprise anybody who was familiar with the ENB material. However, they provide a useful summary view of what is typically written about countries. Further, since they relate directly to surface forms in the text, they may be valuable for guiding further quantitative analyses, e.g. by pinpointing where significant expressions of country positions, arguments and affinities are to be found.

1. (COUNTRY ((supported|opposed) by) COUNTRY)
2. (COUNTRY (said|noted|recommended|explained|responded|stressed| questioned|addressed|reiterated| reported|urged|amended|invited…)); *the equivalence class contains 51 words*
3. (COUNTRY ((clarified|urged|reported) that)
4. (COUNTRY ((presented|demanded|outlined|favored (the|a))
5. (to (apply|safeguard|undertake|link|deliver…)); *the equivalence class contains 63 words*
6. (the (merit|cost effectiveness| merits|importance|idea…) of); *the equivalence class contains 84 words*
7. ((COUNTRY (noted|said|questioned|…)) (the (merit|cost effectiveness| merits|importance|idea…) of))
8. (COUNTRY expressed ((disappointment|concern) that)|((support|appreciation) for)|((readiness|willingness) to)|(satisfaction (with the) (outcome|reconstitution|functioning|work) (of the)))
9. (COUNTRY called (((for |on) (parties|(developed countries)) to)|((for a) (cautious|three phased|common|phased|bottom up|budget|global) approach to)|(for an (overview|elaboration|analysis|evaluation|examination) of)))
10. (COUNTRY highlighted ((the (need|basis) for)|(the (benefits|possibility|establishment) of)|(the (consideration|impact|impacts) of)|(the (use|involvement) of)|((the need to) (err|focus) on)|(the (role|importance) (of the))))

Table 1: Ten of the patterns automatically induced from Earth Negotiations Bulletin texts.

## 4 Using selected information structures

Here we describe our first steps in using some of the induced structures to infer coalitions (4.1) and to scale negotiation positions (4.2).

### 4.1 Dyads of support and opposition

The pattern '(COUNTRY ((supported|opposed) by) COUNTRY)', cf. Table 1, was used as a regular expression to extract instances where relations between countries were recorded with respect to stated positions. This gave 1145 instances of support, and 592 of opposition, often involving multiple countries; recall that 'COUNTRY' may stand for a list of countries. A count was made for each pair of countries in support and opposition, with a distinction made between 'C1 supported by C2' and 'C2 supported by C1'. Figure 1 is a scatterplot made from these counts. It shows, for example, that the US very often finds its statements supported by Canada. Further, whilst the US tends to support the EU relatively often, the EU supports the US only about as often as it opposes the US.

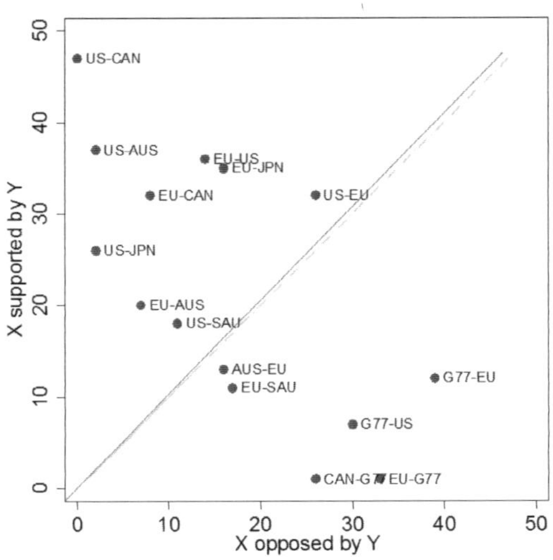


Figure 1: Dyads of support and opposition

### 4.2 Scaling negotiation positions

Patterns 2-4 from Table 1 were combined into a regular expression to extract instances of the statements made by countries. For each country a file was made with the text following every instance of 'COUNTRY said | noted | recommended | (etc.)', until the end of the sentence. The collection of country files was then analyzed with Wordfish (Slapin and Proksch, 2008): this tool, which implements a scaling model, positions texts (here reflecting countries) on a political/ideological dimension based on the relative frequency of discriminating words.

For the 40 countries with the most statements, the parameter indicating country position on the induced dimension ranged in ascending order from Austria (-2.38) via Belgium, Germany, the UK, Switzerland, the US, Canada, Australia, Norway, France, Russia, New Zealand to Japan (-.62) and on to Papua New Guinea (-.26), Tuvalu, Peru, Mexico, Brazil, Argentina, Malaysia, South Korea, Colombia, Saudi Arabia, Chile, Kuwait, Nigeria, Grenada, Uganda, Bangladesh, China, Egypt, the Philippines, South Africa, Indonesia, Venezuela, Iran, Bolivia, Barbados, India and Algeria (1.44).

The method thus perfectly identifies the main cleavage in international climate negotiations between developed and developing countries (cf. Castro et al., 2014). The bifurcation is robust to alternative specifications. Among the ten most discriminating lemmas used by developing countries are 'equal', 'distribut', 'resourc', 'histor', and 'equiti', suggesting an emphasis on fairness and rich countries' historical emissions.

## 5 Closing Remarks

The novel use of a grammar induction algorithm was successful in elucidating the content of a corpus in a complementary way to bag-of-words techniques: some of the induced structures were useful for guiding subsequent analyses as part of a data-driven approach to computational social science. Specifically, in this case, the structures facilitated text analysis at the statement level, i.e. statements about country relations and countries' positions. This meant we could plot country relations and scale country positions even though our source texts were not organized by country.

Given its inherent portability, we see the potential for applying the grammar induction approach to many other corpora, most obviously the other 32 ENB volumes, and other texts with similarly restricted content and style, e.g. parliamentary proceedings. It remains a largely open question as to what happens when the text input becomes more heterogeneous, but see Salway and Touileb (2014) regarding the processing of blog posts.

In ongoing work we are seeking to understand more about how the parameters of the ADIOS algorithm, and the modifications we make, affect the set of structures that it identifies. Also we are considering evaluation metrics to validate the induced patterns and to measure recall.

## Acknowledgements

We are very grateful to Zach Solan for providing an implementation of the ADIOS algorithm, and to Knut Hofland for his help in creating our corpus of ENB texts. This research was supported by a grant from The Research Council of Norway's VERDIKT program.

## References

Stefanie Bailer. 2012. Strategy in the climate change negotiations: do democracies negotiate differently? *Climate Policy* 12(5): 534-551.

Paula Castro, Lena Hörnlein, and Katharina Michaelowa. 2014. Constructed peer groups and path dependence in international organizations. *Global Environmental Change*.

Arianna D'Ulizia, Fernando Ferri and Patrizia Grifoni. 2011. A survey of grammatical inference methods for natural language learning. *Artificial Intelligence Review* 36(1):1-27.

Oren Etzioni, Michele Banko, Stephen Soderland and Daniel S. Weld. Open Information Extraction from the Web. *Comms. of the ACM* 51(12): 68-74.

Justin Grimmer and Brandon M. Stewart. 2013. Text as Data: The Promise and Pitfalls of Automatic Content Analysis Methods for Political Texts. *Political Analysis* 21(3):267-297.

Zellig Harris. 1954. Distributional Structure. *Word* 10(2/3):146-162.

Zellig Harris. 1988. *Language and Information*. Columbia University Press, New York.

Eileen Riloff. 1996. Automatically Generating Extraction Patterns from Untagged Text. *Procs. 13th National Conference on Artificial Intelligence (AAAI-96)*:1044-1049.

Andrew Salway and Samia Touileb. 2014. Applying Grammar Induction to Text Mining. To appear in *Procs. ACL 2014*.

Satoski Sekine. 2006. On-Demand Information Extraction. *Procs. COLING/ACL 2006*: 731-738.

Jonathan Slapin and Sven-Oliver Proksch. 2008. A Scaling Model for Estimating Time-Series Party Positions from Texts. *American Journal of Political Science* 52(3):705-722.

Zach Solan, David Horn, Eytan Ruppin, and Shimon Edelman. 2005. Unsupervised learning of natural languages. *PNAS* 102(33):11629-11634.

Florian Weiler. 2012. Determinants of bargaining success in the climate change negotiations. *Climate Policy* 12(5):552-574.

# Information density, Heaps' Law, and perception of factiness in news

**Miriam Boon**
Technology and Social Behavior, Northwestern University
Evanston, IL 60208, USA
MiriamBoon2012@u.northwestern.edu

## Abstract

Seeking information online can be an exercise in time wasted wading through repetitive, verbose text with little actual content. Some documents are more densely populated with factoids (fact-like claims) than others. The densest documents are potentially the most efficient use of time, likely to include the most information. Thus some measure of "factiness" might be useful to readers. Based on crowdsourced ratings of the factual content of 772 online news articles, we find that after controlling for widely varying document length using Heaps' Law, a significant positive correlation exists between perceived factual content and relative information entropy.

## 1 Introduction

In today's information-based society, finding accurate information is of concern to everyone. There are many obstacles to this goal. Not all people are equally skilled at judging the veracity of a factoid (a term used here to indicate something that is stated as a fact, but that may or may not actually be true.). Nor is it always easy to find the single drop of content you need amidst the oceans of the Internet. Even for those equipped with both skill and access, time is always a limiting factor.

It is this last problem with which this paper is concerned. How can we identify content that most efficiently conveys the most information, given that any information seeker's time is limited?

### 1.1 The difficulty with factoids

Imagine that we must select from a set of documents those that efficiently convey the most information in the fewest words possible; that is, those with the highest factoid rate, $count(factoids)/count(words)$. A human doing this by hand would count the factoids and words in each document. Automating this exact approach would require 'teaching' the computer to identify unique factoids in a document, which requires being able to recognize and discard redundant factoids, which requires at least a rudimentary understanding of each factoid's meaning. These are all difficult tasks for a computer.

Luckily, to achieve our goal, we don't need to know which sentences are factoids. What we need is a good heuristic estimate of information density that computers can easily calculate.

### 1.2 Linking vocabulary to factoids

To insert new information into a text, an author must add words, making the document longer. While the new information can sometimes be conveyed using the same vocabulary as the rest of the text, if the information is sufficiently different from what is already present, it will also likely introduce new vocabulary words.

The result is that the introduction of a new factoid into a text is likely to also introduce new vocabulary, unless it is redundant. Thus, the more non-redundant factoids a text contains, the more varied the vocabulary of the text is likely to be.

### 1.3 From vocabulary to relative entropy

Vocabulary is commonly used in connection with Shannon's information entropy to measure such things as surprisal, redundancy, perplexity, and, of course, information density (Shannon, 1949; McFarlane et al., 2009).

Entropy models text as being created via a Markov process. In its most basic form, it can be written as:

$$H = -K \sum_{i=0}^{L} p_i log_2 p_i \qquad (1)$$

where K is a constant chosen based on the units, L is the length of the document, and $p_i$ is the probability of the $i^{th}$ word. This equation works



*Proceedings of the ACL 2014 Workshop on Language Technologies and Computational Social Science*, pages 33–37,
Baltimore, Maryland, USA, June 26, 2014. 

equally well whether it is used for unigrams, bigrams, or trigrams.

Consider for a moment the relationship between entropy and length, vocabulary, and the probability of each vocabulary word. Entropy increases as both document length and vocabulary increase. Words with lower probability increase entropy more than those with higher probabilities. For this study, probabilities were calculated based on corpus-wide frequencies. This means that, in theory, a large number of the words in a document could have very low probability.

Given two documents of equal length on the same topic, only one of which is rich in information, we might wonder why the information-poor document is, relatively speaking, so long or the information-rich document is so short. This can be explained by noting that: 1. "translation" into simpler versions of a language often leads to a longer text, 2. simple versions of languages generally consist of the most common words in that language, and 3. words that are less common often have more specific, information-dense, complex meanings. Similarly, inefficient word choices typically make excessive use of highly probable function words, which do not increase the entropy as much as less common words. Thus, we can expect the entropy to be higher for the denser document.

### 1.4 Controlling for document length with Heaps' Law

While entropy may not rise as fast with the repetition or addition of highly probable words, however, every word added does still increase the entropy. This follows naturally from the fact that for every word added, another term is added to the summation. We can try to compensate by dividing by document length. But dividing by document length doesn't remove this dependency. I propose that this is because, as Heap's Law tells us, the vocabulary used in a document has a positive relationship with document size (Heaps, 1978). To control for this effect, I fit a curve for unigrams, bigrams, and trigrams to create a model for these relationships; an example can be seen in Figure 1.

I then used that model to calculate the expected document length, expected entropy, and relative entropy, as follows:

$$L_{exp} = 10^{(log_{10}v - b)/m} \quad (2)$$

$$H_{exp} = H\frac{L_{exp}}{L} \quad (3)$$

$$H_{rel} = \frac{H}{H_{exp}} \quad (4)$$

Here the subscript 'exp' stands for 'expected' and the subscript 'rel' for 'relative.' This calculation eliminates the dependency on document length.

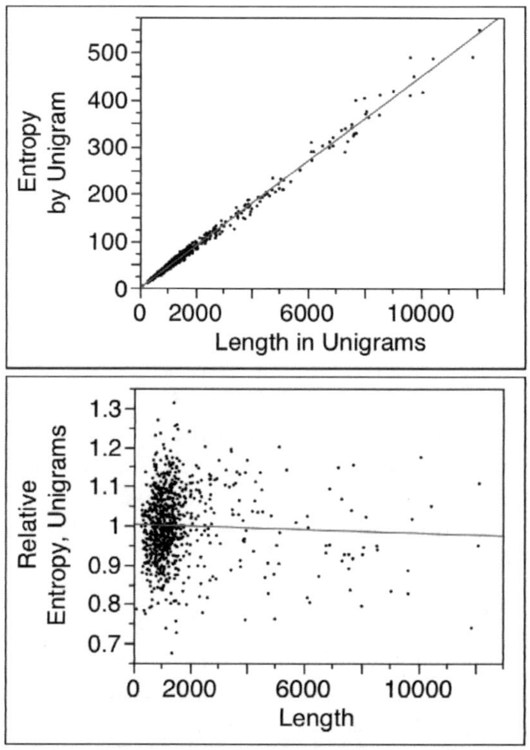


Figure 1: Top: As you can see there is a strong relationship between document length and entropy. $R^2$=0.992, $p > F$: $< 0.0001$. Bottom: Relative entropy, which controls for that relationship, no longer has a significant nor strong relationship with document length. $R^2$=0.0017, $p > F$: 0.2425

## 2 Data and Analysis

To further pursue the hypothesis that residual entropy could be used to identify news articles with lots of factoids, and thus, a sense of 'factiness,' a labeled data set is necessary. Lots of websites allow users to rate articles, but those ratings don't have anything to do with the presence of factoids. Labeling a data set of adequate size by hand would be tedious, time-consuming, and costly.

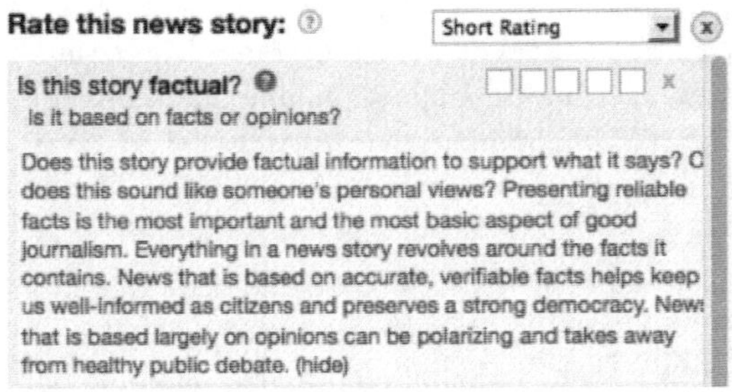


Figure 2: Mousing over the question makes the text "Is it based on facts or opinions?" appear in pale grey text. Clicking on the question mark icon next to the question, "Is this story factual?" reveals an explanation of what the user should be rating.

### 2.1 Crowdsourcing with NewsTrust

Fortunately, a project called NewsTrust provided a feasible alternative. NewsTrust, founded in 2005 by Fabrice Florin, created four sets of specific review questions designed to inspire reviewers to think critically about the quality of articles they review. NewsTrust partnered with independent academic researchers Cliff Lampe and Kelly Garrett to validate the review questions. They jointly administered a survey in which respondents were asked to complete one of the review instruments regarding either the original version of an article or blog post, or a degraded version.

The independent study found that even the less experienced, less knowledgeable readers were able to distinguish between the two versions of the story. The shortest review instrument, with only one question, had the most discriminating power, while the slightly longer normative review instrument (which added five more questions) yielded responses from non-experts that most closely matched those of NewsTrust's expert journalists (Lampe and Garrett, 2007; Florin et al., 2006; Florin, 2009).

Using their validated survey instrument, NewsTrust created a system that allowed users to read articles elsewhere, rate them using one of the four review instruments, and even rate other NewsTrust users' reviews of articles. Each user has a trustworthiness rating (which can be bolstered by becoming validated as a journalist expert), and each article has a composite rating, a certainty level for that rating, reviews, and ratings of reviews.

One of the dimensions of journalistic quality for which NewsTrust users rate articles is called 'facts'. This can be taken as an aspect of "factiness": the extent to which people perceived the article as truthful and factual. It follows that, to the extent that the users are making a good-faith attempt to rate articles based on facts regardless of the soundness of their judgment about what is or is not true, articles with a high rating for 'facts' should have more factoids, and therefore a higher density of information.

### 2.2 Data acquisition

When this research project was launched, NewsTrust had recently been acquired by the Poynter Institute. Although they were open to making their data available for research purposes, they were not yet able to access the data in order to do so. Instead, the review data for over 11000 stories from NewsTrust's political section were retrieved using Python, Requests, and Beautiful Soup. A combination of Alchemy API, digital library archives, and custom scrapers for 19 different publication websites were used to harvest the corresponding article texts.

It quickly became clear, however, that it would not be possible to completely capture all 11,000 articles. Some of the independent blogs and websites no longer existed. Others had changed their link structure, making it difficult to find the correct article. A great deal of content was behind paywalls, or simply did not have a webpage structure that lent itself to clean extraction. As the text would be used for automated analysis, it was essential that the extracted text be as clean of detritus as possible. As a result, the dataset shrank from a potential 11,000 rated articles to only 3300 for which I could be confident of having clean text. Approximately 2600 of those articles have been rated by at least one NewsTrust user based on factiness, and after removing any with fewer than four facts ratings, the data set shrank further to only 805[1] articles. Unigrams, bigrams, and trigrams were extracted from these articles using the Natural Language Toolkit, NLTK; all text was lowercased, and only alphanumeric words were included.

### 2.3 Analysis

The relationship between length and vocabulary was modeled using the optimize toolkit from SciPy, and visualized with MatPlotLib. The result-

[1]One outlier document was removed.

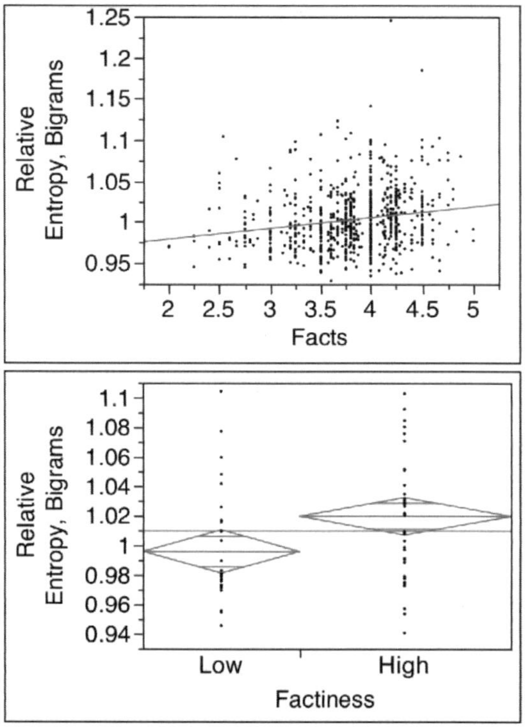


Figure 3: Top: Bivariate fit for bigrams. Bottom: Oneway ANOVA for bigrams.

ing relationship was used to calculate the relative entropy for each document.

For bivariate analysis, 772 of these documents could be used[2]. But for the oneway analysis, documents needed to be separated into two distinct clusters. We used Weka's K-Means clustering algorithm to find the location of three clusters. The 90% confidence interval for each article (calculated using the invididual user ratings for 'facts') was used to determine cluster membership. That is, articles for which that confidence interval would overlap with both the upper and lower cluster were discarded (738 documents in total). This process was repeated for 80 and 85% confidence levels; they yielded more data points (198 and 458), a higher level of significance, and a lower $R^2$. A 95% confidence level did not yield enough articles with a low facts rating to analyze.

## 3 Results and Discussion

The bivariate analysis showed a small but significant positive relationship between factual rating and relative entropy as calculated for unigrams, bigrams, and to a lesser extent, trigrams. The results can be seen in Table 1 and Figure 3. These relationships strengthened according to the ANOVA for the more distinct high and low factiness classifications.

If we accept the assumption that the articles rated by NewsTrust users as highly factual will contain a higher density of factoids, then this result supports the hypothesis that relative entropy is positively correlated with that characteristic. Conversely, if we accept the assumption that entropy should be correlated with factoid density, then this result supports the claim that NewsTrust users effectively identify articles that are more information dense. Future work on the fact-rated sub-

| | **Unigram** | **Bigram** | **Trigram** |
|---|---|---|---|
| Bivar. $R^2$ | 0.033 | 0.032 | 0.014 |
| $p > F$ | $< 0.0001$ | $< 0.0001$ | $< 0.0008$ |
| Oneway $R^2$ | 0.086 | 0.084 | 0.082 |
| $p > \|t\|$ | 0.0154 | 0.0163 | 0.0178 |

Table 1: Bivariate analysis (n = 772) and Oneway ANOVA (n = 68).

corpus has two obvious directions. First, and most closely related to the work described in this paper, is the goal of proving either assumption in a more controlled experiment. If one of these assumptions can be supported, then it strengthens the claim about the other, which will be interesting from both a linguistic perspective, and a human-computer interaction perspective. The other avenue of inquiry that follows naturally from this work is to look for other textual features that might, in combination, enable the automatic prediction of fact ratings based on article text.

## Acknowledgments

This work was partly supported by the Technology and Social Behavior program at Northwestern University, the National Science Foundation, the Knight Foundation, and Google. Many thanks to Dr. Darren Gergle for his insight on the larger NewsTrust data set, to Dr. Janet Pierrehumbert for her guidance on entropy and factiness, and to Dr. Larry Birnbaum for his intellectual guidance as well as his assistance on this paper.

[2] 33 documents with particularly low confidence levels for their rating were removed

## References


Fabrice Florin, Cliff Lampe, and Kelly Garrett. 2006. Survey report summary - NewsTrust.

Fabrice Florin. 2009. NewsTrust communications 2009 report. Technical report.

Harold Stanley Heaps. 1978. *Information retrieval: Computational and theoretical aspects*. Academic Press, Inc.

Cliff Lampe and R. Kelly Garrett. 2007. It's all news to me: The effect of instruments on ratings provision. In *System Sciences, 2007. HICSS 2007. 40th Annual Hawaii International Conference on*, page 180b180b.

Delano J. McFarlane, Noemie Elhadad, and Rita Kukafka. 2009. Perplexity analysis of obesity news coverage. *AMIA Annual Symposium Proceedings*, 2009:426–430. 00001.

Claude E. Shannon. 1949. *The mathematical theory of communication*. Urbana, University of Illinois Press.

# Measuring the Public Accountability of New Modes of Governance

**Bruno Wueest**
Institute of Political Science
University of Zurich
wueest@ipz.uzh.ch

**Michael Amsler**
Institute of Computational Linguistics
University of Zurich
mamsler@ifi.uzh.ch

**Gerold Schneider**
Institute of Computational Linguistics
University of Zurich
gschneid@ifi.uzh.ch

## Abstract

We present an encompassing research endeavour on the public accountability of new modes of governance in Europe. The aim of this project is to measure the salience, tonality and framing of regulatory bodies and public interest organisations in newspaper coverage and parliamentary debates over the last 15 years. In order to achieve this, we use language technology which is still underused in political science text analyses. Institutionally, the project has emerged from a collaboration between a computational linguistics and a political science department.

## 1 Introduction

The institutionalization of the regulatory state in Europe entailed new modes of governance such as transgovernmental networks between officials and non-state authorities or the involvement of private corporations (e.g. rating agencies) in the policy processes (Gilardi, 2005; Abbott and Snidal, 2008). At the subnational level, the emergence of regulatory agencies and public-private partnerships spreading across metropolitan regions have come to challenge traditional state institutions (Kelleher and Lowery, 2009). Since these new modes of governance organize political authority along functional rather than territorial lines, many observers are worried about their potential "democratic deficit" (Dahl, 1994; Follesdal and Hix, 2006; Keohane et al., 2009). In response to these considerations, scholars usually point to the administrative and professional accountability mechanisms of governmental and parliamentary oversight as well as judicial review (Majone, 2000; Lodge, 2002; Busuioc, 2009). Other, more informal accountability mechanisms such as media coverage and public involvement, in contrast, have been either neglected, dismissed as scarcely relevant or dealt with only in comparative case studies (Maggetti, 2012). This is surprising, given that public communication plays an ever more decisive role for setting the political agenda and establishing transparency of policy making in modern democratic societies (Walgrave et al., 2008; Koopmans and Statham, 2010; Müller, forthcoming). With respect to the public accountability of new modes of governance, the media can thus be expected to constitute a key intermediary variable for the progressive formalization and institutionalization of voluntary private rules through reputational mechanisms (Gentzkow and Shapiro, 2006).

This paper is structured as follows. In section 2 we present our core research question, in section 3 we summarize our research methods, and in section 4 we briefly present a pilot study.

## 2 Research Question

It is important to ask whether and to what extent public communication systematically exposes new modes of governance to public accountability. More precisely, the project's ambition is to determine how much attention the media and parliamentary debates dedicate to survey the regulatory bodies and public interest organizations under scrutiny, whether they watch these actors critically, and whether they report on these actors in terms of frames which are conductive to their public accountability, e.g. norm and rule compliance, transparency, efficiency or responsiveness to public demands.



*Proceedings of the ACL 2014 Workshop on Language Technologies and Computational Social Science*, pages 38–43,
Baltimore, Maryland, USA, June 26, 2014. 

## 3 Methodology

To answer these questions, the project implements approaches developed in computational linguistics and web automation in order to collect and classify big text data at the European level (European and internationally relevant newspapers), the domestic level in four countries (newspapers in the U.K., France, Germany and Switzerland), and the subnational level in eight metropolitan areas (parliamentary debates and newspapers relevant for London, Birmingham, Paris, Lyon, Berlin, Stuttgart, Berne and Zurich). The project (1) starts from an encompassing gazetteer of actors involved in the new modes of governance in the areas and countries mentioned above, (2) uses application programming interfaces (API) and webscraping techniques to establish a large representative text corpus in English, French and German, (3) calculates the salience of the actors of interest by means of named entity recognition, coreference resolution and keyword detection, (4) applies sentiment detection and opinion mining to estimate the tonality of these actors, (5) uses relation mining methods (Schneider et al., 2009) to detect interactions and types of interactions between the entities of interest, and (6) intends to automate the recognition of media frames used in the context of these actors by identifying hidden topics via latent semantic analysis (LSA) (McFarlane, 2011; Odijk et al., 2014).

As points 3-6 provide key research challenges, we will discuss them in more detail in the following subsections. Before that, we present an overview of our current pipeline.

### 3.1 Pipeline

The pipeline consists of several components chained together in a modular way (see Figure 1). This provides us with the possibility to exchange components on demand. First, data acquisition is done via the use of an API to the media content database (e.g. LexisNexis). This allows us to fully automate the retrieval and storage of the media documents.

At a second stage, we employ a full natural language processing chain which includes morphological analysis, tagging, lemmatizing, and dependency parsing. On this basis, we then conduct several more layers of analysis. On the one hand, we use the result of the preprocessing chain for coreference resolution and sentiment analysis as well as relation mining. On the other hand, we also integrate further tools such as named entity recognition and LSA which can be applied on the full text or corpus level. The thus enriched data is then aggregated and stored in a database.

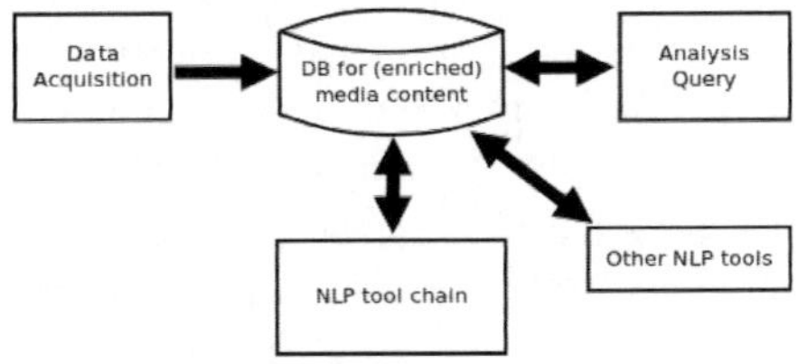


Figure 1: Scheme of pipeline

Finally, the actual data analysis can be conducted by querying the database, based on the already available information or an adapted setting suitable to the requirements of the media content analysis.

### 3.2 Salience, Named Entities and Coreferences

One of the main metrics of interest is the salience of the entities. Therefore, a reliable detection of the entities in the articles is a pivotal task. Furthermore it is crucial to find those occurences of entities in the text which are not directly detectable by using a gazetter, since journalists often use references to the entities in the same article. Hence, we will integrate coreference resolution (Klenner and Tuggener, 2011) into our pipeline. In addition, we will also create a resource which will allow us to integrate external information on the entities, thus increasing the performance of the coreference resolution. For example, politicians are often mentioned with their name, their function (e.g. National Council), their party affiliation, their age, or a combination of such attributes. Together with the metadata of the media documents (media source, and time of publication) it is then possible to calculate these attributes and possible combinations and include them in the coreference resolution module in order to increase both precision and recall.

### 3.3 From Sentiment Detection to Opinion Mining

Sentiment analysis and opinion mining are research areas in computational linguistics which have received growing attention in the last decade (Pang and Lee, 2008; Liu and Zhang, 2012). In order to detect the tonality in the media coverage towards the actors under scrutiny, we use a lexicon-based compositional sentiment analysis system component similar to Taboada et al. (2011). However, our approach is additionally based on the output of the full dependency parse and the results of the named entity recognition and coreference resolution. This will provide us with the ability to perform target-specific tonality calculation.

In addition to the mere calculation of sentiment or tonality over a whole article, our task includes the detection of sentiment on the sentence level and in respect to certain targets (i.e. entities). An additional challenge is to detect quotations including their sources and targets, since they may reveal the actors' most opinionated stances towards each other (Balahur et al., 2009). From this perspective, opinion mining can be seen as a sister discipline to sentiment analysis, which we can employ to map utterances of actors towards other actors, or towards specific political topics, stepping from classical sentiment detection to relation and opinion mining. We will focus on high precision assignment of the source of the statement.

It is important to note that the detection and determination of sentiment and opinion in media documents is a challenging endeavour since it differs in many ways from the task of previous research which has mostly considered reviews and other clearly opinionated text (Balahur et al., 2010). It will therefore also be necessary to adapt the sentiment analysis system to the domain of (political) news text and to use advanced techniques to match fine-grained targets and the entity to which they belong. For example, it should be possible to assign statements of a spokesperson to the institution he or she represents. However, we can build on existing research, since such a mapping can be considered similar to aspect-based opinion mining (Zhang and Liu, 2014).

### 3.4 Relation Mining

In well-resourced areas such as biomedical relation mining, the detection of interactions between entities such as genes and proteins or drugs and diseases is an established research focus. Training resources are abundant, and several systems have been evaluated in competitive challenges. Political science texts are typically less richly annotated. However, it is also possible to learn patterns expressing interactions from lean document-level annotation, by using distance-learning methods. If a document is annotated as containing the key actors A and B, then all syntactic connections found in that document between A and B can be assumed to provide patterns typically expressing interactions. Such approaches have been used in biomedicine (Rinaldi et al., 2012) and can be ported to the political domain.

### 3.5 Media Frames

Associative Framing (van Atteveldt et al., 2008) is based on measuring co-occurrence in large context windows. His suggested association measure is also different, he uses the conditional probability of seeing concept 1 ($c1$) in the context of concept 2 ($c2$), $p(c1|c2)$. Sahlgren (2006) describes how short context windows tend to detect syntagmatic relations like collocations, while large context windows detect paradigmatic relations. In van Atteveldt et al. (2008), concepts are basically keywords, while we will use vector space models, which allow one to automatically detect concepts. In vector space model approaches, each word is defined by the sum of its contexts, and words which have very similar contexts are clustered into a concept. There are many variants of this approach: in singular-value decomposition (SVD) or latent semantic analysis (LSA) approaches (Deerwester et al., 1990), the original very high dimensional space is reduced to fewer dimensions. In Word Space (Schütze, 1998) each word is defined recursively, by the contexts of its contexts, using an observation window of up to 100 words before and after the target word. Rothenhäusler and Schütze (2009) have shown that approaches using syntactic relations instead of large context windows can even perform better.

In the political communication literature, the definition of frames is contested. Matthes and Kohring (2008) thus suggest a bottom-up, data-driven and interactive method which on the one hand offers the possibility to correct and guide automatic approaches as has been exemplified by Hu et al. (2011), on the other hand the rigid consistency of automatic approaches can also add new insights for data interpretation.

## 4 Pilot Study

As a short glimpse at the potential of our research we present first data from a small pilot study. The depth of the analysis is still limited due to the not yet fully functional pipeline. In a first step, we collected 4445 articles from the last ten years in three large German print and online news sources. The institutions under scrutiny are (private) associations for technical inspection in Germany. In this area, the TÜV (Technischer Überwachungsverein, i.e., Technical Inspection Association) and its subcompanies almost exert a regulatory monopoly. As a first goal, we want to investigate the difference in the tonality in the media coverage towards the institutions in this area. We therefore chose to investigate a public scandal revolving on defective breast implants that have been tested and certified by a TÜV subcompany. Table 1 reports the results.

| Institution | Articles | Tonality | | | |
|---|---|---|---|---|---|
| Name | n | negative | ambivalent | neutral | positive |
| TÜV | 57 | 47 | 5 | 3 | 2 |
| TÜV subcompanies | 45 | 39 | 3 | 2 | 1 |
| Other institutions | 10 | 6 | 2 | 0 | 2 |

Table 1: Absolute counts of articles about breast implants and tonality per institution

A first interesting finding is that we only found articles about breast implants in the last 3 years. Considering the sentiment analysis results for these articles, we see a clearly negative aggregated result. 82.1% of the articles were of negative tonality, compared to only 4.5% positive tonality. The remaining articles were of neutral (4.5%) or ambivalent (8.9%) tonality. The percentage of negative articles is even larger if only articles containing mentions of TÜV and its subcompanies are considered (84.3%), while the percentage of positive articles drops to 2.9%.

Furthermore, these findings are in line with the increase in negative articles on TÜV subcompanies during these years (see Figure 2). In fact, from all negative articles about the TÜV subcompanies, 28.8% in 2012 and even 38.2% in 2013 contained mentions of breast implants. The scandal itself was therefore responsible for the increase in negative articles in this period.

This development can be interpreted as an indication for the accountability of such institutions in the public media, although it remains an open question which aspects were dominant in the public discourse considering the scandal about the breast implants.

In sum, this pilot study increases our confidence to be able to successfully collect the necessary data for our main purpose, i.e. to answer the question whether new forms of governance are held accountable in the media. In the near future, we

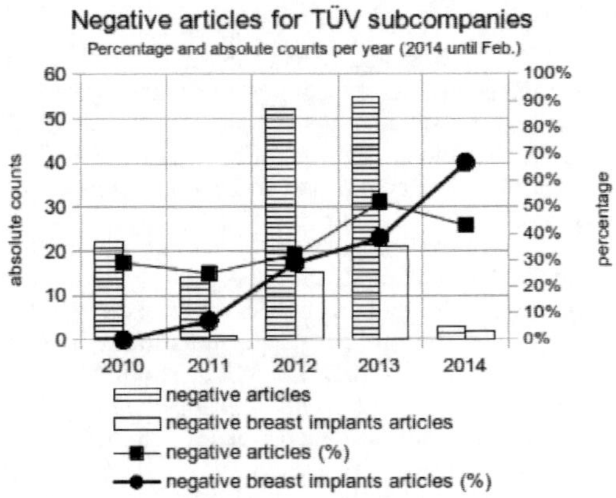


Figure 2: Percentage and raw counts of negative (breast implant) articles for TÜV subcompanies

plan to implement approaches that allow us to inductively detect the issues brought forward in the context of an actor in a selection of texts. More precisely, we are planning to describe and detect the dynamics of the debate in articles as well as the tonality inside them.

## 5 Conclusions

We have introduced a project measuring media coverage and applying opinion and relation mining to the question of accountability of new modes of governance in Europe. To answer how public communication exposes them to public accountability, we apply computational linguistics methods ranging from named entity recognition, dependency parsing and coreference resolution to opinion and relation mining and ultimately framing.

We have given a pilot study on a public scandal involving defective breast implants that have been tested and certified by a TÜV subcompany in Germany. We find, on the one hand, that most of the articles on breast implants during the period are of negative tonality, and on the other hand, that a corresponding proportion of negative articles on TÜV mentions breast implants, explaining the spike in negativity. In future research, we will detect such spikes in a data-driven fashion and with the help of targeted opinion and relation mining approaches.

## Acknowledgments

This research is supported by the Swiss National Science Foundation project NCCR democracy[1].

[1] http://www.nccr-democracy.uzh.ch

## References


Kenneth W. Abbott and Duncan Snidal. 2008. The governance triangle: regulatory standards institutions and the shadow of the state. In Walter Mattli and Ngaire Woods, editors, *The Politics of Global Regulation*. Princeton University Press, Princeton, NJ.

Alexandra Balahur, Ralf Steinberger, Erik van der Goot, Bruno Pouliquen, and Mijail Kabadjov. 2009. Opinion mining on newspaper quotations. In *Proceedings of the 2009 IEEE/WIC/ACM International Joint Conference on Web Intelligence and Intelligent Agent Technology-Volume 03*, pages 523–526. IEEE Computer Society.

Alexandra Balahur, Ralf Steinberger, Mijail Kabadjov, Vanni Zavarella, Erik van der Goot, Matina Halkia, Bruno Pouliquen, and Jenya Belyaeva. 2010. Sentiment analysis in the news. In *Proceedings of the Seventh conference on International Language Resources and Evaluation (LREC'10)*, Valletta, Malta, may.

Madalina Busuioc. 2009. Accountability, control and independence: the case of European agencies. *European Law Journal*, 15:599–615.

Robert A. Dahl. 1994. A democratic dilemma: System effectiveness versus citizen participation. *Political Science Quarterly*, 109(1):23–34.

Scott Deerwester, Susan T. Dumais, George W. Furnas, Thomas K. Landauer, and Richard Harshman. 1990. Indexing by latent semantic analysis. *Journal of the American Society of Information Science*, 41(6):391–407.

Andreas Follesdal and Simon Hix. 2006. Why there is a democratic deficit in the EU: A response to Majone and Moravcsik. *JCMS: Journal of Common Market Studies*, 44:533–562.

Matthiew Gentzkow and Jesse M. Shapiro. 2006. Media bias and reputation. *Journal of Political Economy*, 114(2):280–316.

Fabrizio Gilardi. 2005. The institutional foundations of regulatory capitalism: The diffusion of independent regulatory agencies in Western Europe. *Annals of the American Academy of Political and Social Science*, 598:84–101.

Yuening Hu, Jordan Boyd-Graber, and Brianna Satinoff. 2011. Interactive topic modeling. In *Proceedings of the 49th Annual Meeting of the Association for Computational Linguistics: Human Language Technologies*, pages 248–257, Portland, Oregon, USA, June. Association for Computational Linguistics.

Christine A. Kelleher and David Lowery. 2009. Central city size, metropolitan institutions and political participation. *British Journal of Political Science*, 39(1):59–92.

Robert O. Keohane, Stephen Macedo, and Andrew Moravcsik. 2009. Democracy-enhancing multilateralism. *International Organization*, 63(1):1–31.

Manfred Klenner and Don Tuggener. 2011. An incremental entity-mention model for coreference resolution with restrictive antecedent accessibility. In G Angelova, K Bontcheva, R Mitkov, and N Nikolov, editors, *Recent Advances in Natural Language Processing (RANLP 2011)*, Proceedings of Recent Advances in Natural Language Processing, pages 178–185, September.

Ruud Koopmans and Paul Statham. 2010. *The Making of a European Public Sphere. Media Discourse and Political Contention*. Cambridge University Press, Cambridge, MA.

Bing Liu and Lei Zhang. 2012. A survey of opinion mining and sentiment analysis. In *Mining Text Data*, pages 415–463. Springer.

Martin Lodge. 2002. The wrong type of regulation? regulatory failure and the railways in Britain and Germany. *Journal of Public Policy*, 22:271–297.

Martino Maggetti. 2012. The media accountability of independent regulatory agencies. *European Political Science Review*, 4(3):385–408.

Giandomenico Majone. 2000. The credibility crisis of community regulation. *Journal of Common Market Studies*, 38:273–302.

Jörg Matthes and Matthias Kohring. 2008. The content analysis of media frames: toward improving reliability and validity. *Journal of Communication*, 58:258–279.

Delano J. McFarlane, 2011. *Computational Methods for Analyzing Health News Coverage*. PhD dissertation, Columbia University.

Lisa Müller. forthcoming. *Patterns of Media Performance: Comparing the Contribution of Mass Media to Democratic Quality Worldwide*. Palgrave Macmillan, Houndmills, UK.

Daan Odijk, Bjorn Burscher, Rens Vliegenthart, and Maarten de Rijke, 2014. *Automatic Thematic Content Analysis: Finding Frames in News*. unpub. Ms., Amsterdam, NL.

Bo Pang and Lillian Lee. 2008. Opinion mining and sentiment analysis. *Foundations and trends in information retrieval*, 2(1-2):1–135.

Fabio Rinaldi, Gerold Schneider, and Simon Clematide. 2012. Relation mining experiments in the pharmacogenomics domain. *Journal of Biomedical Informatics*.

Klaus Rothenhäusler and Hinrich Schütze. 2009. Unsupervised classification with dependency based word spaces. In *Proceedings of the Workshop on Geometrical Models of Natural Language Semantics*, pages 17–24, Athens, Greece, March. Association for Computational Linguistics.

Magnus Sahlgren. 2006. *The Word-Space Model: Using distributional Analysis to represent syntagmatic and paradigmatic relations between words in high-dimensional vector spaces.* Ph.D. thesis, Stockholm University.

Gerold Schneider, Kaarel Kaljurand, and Fabio Rinaldi. 2009. Detecting protein-protein interactions in biomedical texts using a parser and linguistic resources. In *Computational Linguistics and Intelligent Text Processing*, volume 5449, pages 406–417, Berlin, DE. CICLing, Springer.

Hinrich Schütze. 1998. Automatic word sense discrimination. *Computational Linguistics*, 24(1):97–124.

Maite Taboada, Julian Brooke, Milan Tofiloski, Kimberly Voll, and Manfred Stede. 2011. Lexicon-based methods for sentiment analysis. *Computational linguistics*, 37(2):267–307.

Wouter van Atteveldt, Jan Kleinnijenhuis, and Nel Ruigrok. 2008. Parsing, semantic networks, and political authority: Using syntactic analysis to extract semantic relations from dutch newspaper articles. *Political Analysis*, 16(4):428–446.

Stefaan Walgrave, Stuart Soroka, and Michiel Nuytemans. 2008. The mass media's political agenda-setting power: A longitudinal analysis of media, parliament, and government in Belgium (1993 to 2000). *Comparative Political Studies*, 41:814–836.

Lei Zhang and Bing Liu. 2014. Aspect and entity extraction for opinion mining. In *Data Mining and Knowledge Discovery for Big Data*, pages 1–40. Springer.

# Optimizing Features in Active Machine Learning for Complex Qualitative Content Analysis

**Jasy Liew Suet Yan**
School of Information Studies
Syracuse University, USA
jliewsue@syr.edu

**Nancy McCracken**
School of Information Studies
Syracuse University, USA
njmccrac@syr.edu

**Shichun Zhou**
College of Engineering and Computer Science
Syracuse University, USA
szhou02@syr.edu

**Kevin Crowston**
National Science Foundation, USA
crowston@syr.edu

## Abstract

We propose a semi-automatic approach for content analysis that leverages machine learning (ML) being initially trained on a small set of hand-coded data to perform a first pass in coding, and then have human annotators correct machine annotations in order to produce more examples to retrain the existing model incrementally for better performance. In this "active learning" approach, it is equally important to optimize the creation of the initial ML model given less training data so that the model is able to capture most if not all positive examples, and filter out as many negative examples as possible for human annotators to correct. This paper reports our attempt to optimize the initial ML model through feature exploration in a complex content analysis project that uses a multidimensional coding scheme, and contains codes with sparse positive examples. While different codes respond optimally to different combinations of features, we show that it is possible to create an optimal initial ML model using only a single combination of features for codes with at least 100 positive examples in the gold standard corpus.

## 1 Introduction

Content analysis, a technique for finding evidence of concepts of theoretical interest through text, is an increasingly popular technique social scientists use in their research investigations. In the process commonly known as "coding", social scientists often have to painstakingly comb through large quantities of natural language corpora to annotate text segments (e.g., phrase, sentence, and paragraphs) with codes exhibiting the concepts of interest (Miles & Huberman, 1994). Analyzing textual data is very labor-intensive, time-consuming, and is often limited to the capabilities of individual researchers (W. Evans, 1996). The coding process becomes even more demanding as the complexity of the project increases especially in the case of attempting to apply a multidimensional coding scheme with a significant number of codes (Dönmez, Rosé, Stegmann, Weinberger, & Fischer, 2005).

With the proliferation and availability of digital texts, it is challenging, if not impossible, for human coders to manually analyze torrents of text to help advance social scientists' understanding of the practices of different populations of interest through textual data. Therefore, computational methods offer significant benefits to help augment human capabilities to explore massive amounts of text in more complex ways for theory generation and theory testing. Content analysis can be framed as a text classification problem, where each text segment is labeled based on a predetermined set of categories or codes.

Full automation of content analysis is still far from being perfect (Grimmer & Stewart, 2013). The accuracy of current automatic approaches on the best performing codes in social science research ranges from 60-90% (Broadwell et al., 2013; Crowston, Allen, & Heckman, 2012; M. Evans, McIntosh, Lin, & Cates, 2007; Ishita, Oard, Fleischmann, Cheng, & Templeton, 2010; Zhu, Kraut, Wang, & Kittur, 2011). While the potential of automatic content analysis is promising, computational methods should not be viewed as a replacement for the role of the primary researcher in the careful interpretation of text. Rather, the computers' pattern recognition capabilities can be leveraged to seek out the most likely examples for each code of interest, thus reducing the amount of texts researchers have to read and process.

We propose a semi-automatic method that promotes a close human-computer partnership for content analysis. Machine learning (ML) is used to perform the first pass of coding on the unlabeled texts. Human annotators then have to correct only what the ML model identifies as positive examples of each code. The initial ML



*Proceedings of the ACL 2014 Workshop on Language Technologies and Computational Social Science*, pages 44–48,
Baltimore, Maryland, USA, June 26, 2014. 

model needs to learn only from a small set of hand-coded examples (i.e., gold standard data), and will evolve and improve as machine annotations that are verified by human annotators are used to incrementally retrain the model. In contrast to conventional machine learning, this "active learning" approach will significantly reduce the amount of training data needed upfront from the human annotators. However, it is still equally important to optimize the creation of the initial ML model given less training data so that the model is able to capture most if not all positive examples, and filter out as many negative examples as possible for human annotators to correct.

To effectively implement the active learning approach for coding qualitative data, we have to first understand the nature and complexity of content analysis projects in social science research. Our pilot case study, an investigation of leadership behaviors exhibited in emails from a FLOSS development project (Misiolek, Crowston, & Seymour, 2012), reveals that it is common for researchers to use a multidimensional coding scheme consisting of a significant number of codes in their research inquiry. Previous work has shown that not all dimensions in a multidimensional coding scheme could be applied fully automatically with acceptable level of accuracy (Dönmez et al., 2005) but little is known if it is possible at all to train an optimal model for all codes using the same combination of features. Also, the distribution of codes is often times uneven with some rarely occurring codes having only few positive examples in the gold standard corpus.

This paper presents our attempt in optimizing the initial ML model through feature exploration using gold standard data created from a multidimensional coding scheme, including codes that suffer from sparseness of positive examples. Specifically, our study is guided by two research questions:

a) *How can features for an initial machine learning model be optimized for all codes in a text classification problem based on multi-dimensional coding schemes? Is it possible to train a one-size-fits-all model for all codes using a single combination of features?*
b) *Are certain features better suited for codes with sparse positive examples?*

## 2 Machine Learning Experiments

To optimize the initial machine learning model, we systematically ran multiple experiments using a gold standard corpus of emails from a free/libre/open-source software (FLOSS) development project coded for leadership behaviors (Misiolek et al., 2012). The coding scheme contained six dimensions: 1) social/relationship, 2) task process, 3) task substance, 4) dual process and substance, 5) change behaviors, and 6) networking. The number of codes for each dimension ranged from 1 to 14. There were a total of 35 codes in the coding scheme. Each sentence could be assigned more than one code. Framing the problem as a multi-label classification task, we trained a binary classification model for each code using support vector machine (SVM) with ten-fold cross-validation. This gold standard corpus consisted of 3,728 hand-coded sentences from 408 email messages.

For the active learning setup, we tune the initial ML model for high recall since having the annotators pick out positive examples that have been incorrectly classified by the model is preferable to missing machine-annotated positive examples to be presented to human annotators for verification (Liew, McCracken, & Crowston, 2014). Therefore, the initial ML model with low precision is acceptable.

| Category | Features |
|---|---|
| Content | Unigram, bigram, pruning, tagging, lowercase, stopwords, stemming, part-of-speech (POS) tags |
| Syntactic | Token count |
| Orthographic | Capitalization of first letter of a word, capitalization of entire word |
| Word list | Subjectivity words |
| Semantic | Role of sender (software developer or not) |

Table 1. Features for ML model.

As shown in Table 1, we have selected general candidate features that have proven to work well across various text classification tasks, as well as one semantic feature specific to the context of FLOSS development projects. For content features, techniques that we have incorporated to reduce the feature space include pruning, substituting certain tokens with more generic tags, converting all tokens to lowercase, excluding stopwords, and stemming. Using the wrapper approach (Kohavi & John, 1997), the same classifier is used to test the prediction performance of various feature combinations listed in Table 1.

| Model | SINGLE | | MULTIPLE | |
|---|---|---|---|---|
| Measure | **Mean Recall** | **Mean Precision** | **Mean Recall** | **Mean Precision** |
| **Overall** | | | | |
| All (35) | 0.690 | 0.065 | 0.877 | 0.068 |
| **Dimension** | | | | |
| Change (1) | 0.917 | 0.011 | 1.000 | 0.016 |
| Dual Process and Substance (13) | 0.675 | 0.069 | 0.852 | 0.067 |
| Networking (1) | 0.546 | 0.010 | 0.843 | 0.020 |
| Process (3) | 0.445 | 0.006 | 0.944 | 0.024 |
| Relationship (14) | 0.742 | 0.083 | 0.872 | 0.089 |
| Substance (3) | 0.735 | 0.061 | 0.919 | 0.051 |

Table 2. Comparison of mean recall and mean precision between SINGLE and MULTIPLE models.

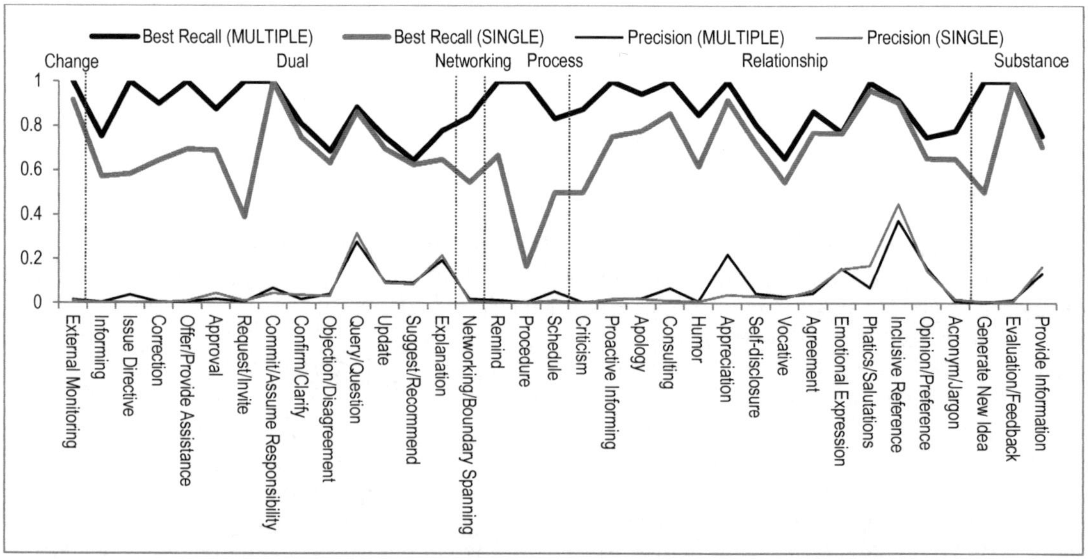


Figure 1. Recall and precision for each code (grouped by dimension).

## 3 Results and Discussion

We ran 343 experiments with different combinations of the 13 features in Table 1. We first compare the performance of the best one-size-fits-all initial machine learning model that produces the highest recall using a single combination of features for all codes (SINGLE) with an "ensemble" model that uses different combinations of features to produce the highest recall for each code (MULTIPLE). The SINGLE model combines content (unigram + bigram + POS tags + lowercase + stopwords) with syntactic, orthographic, and semantic features. None of the best feature combination for each code in the MULTIPLE model coincides with the feature combination in the SINGLE model. For example, the best feature combination for code "Phatics/Salutations" consists of only 2 out of the 13 features (unigram + bigram).

The best feature combination for each code in the MULTIPLE model varies with only some regularity noted in a few codes within the Dual and Substance dimensions. However, these patterns are not consistent across all codes in a single dimension indicating that the pertinent linguistic features for codes belonging to the same dimension may differ despite their conceptual similarities, and even fitting an optimal model for all codes within a single dimension may prove to be difficult especially when the distribution of codes is uneven, and positive examples for certain codes are sparse. There are also no consistent feature patterns observed from the codes with sparse positive examples in the MULTIPLE model.

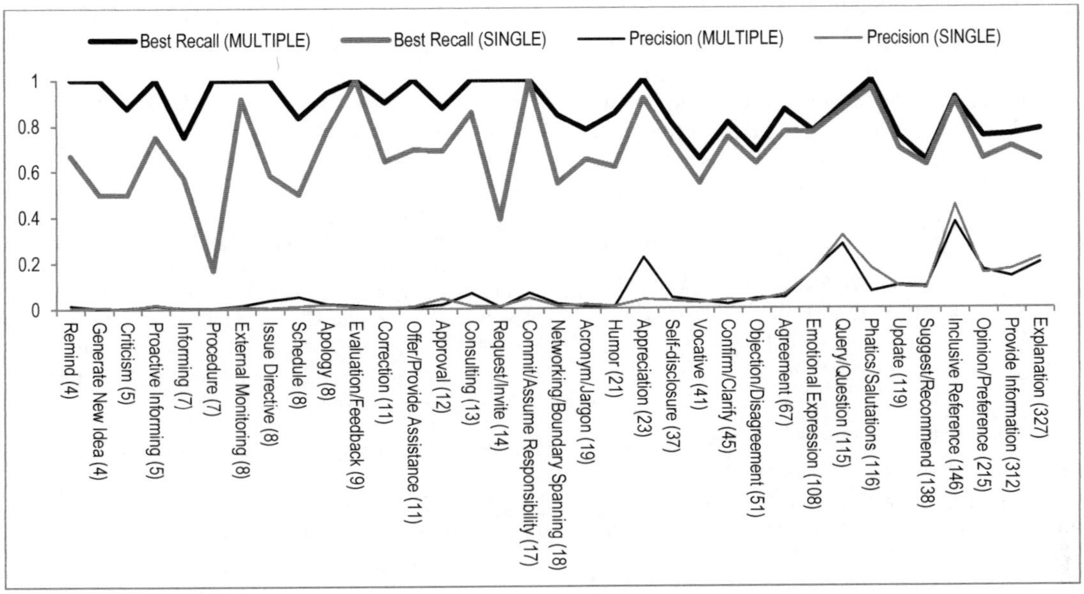


Figure 2. Recall and precision for each code (sorted by gold frequency)

The comparison between the two models in Table 2 further demonstrates that the MULTIPLE model outperforms the SINGLE model both in the overall mean recall of all 35 codes, as well as the mean recall for each dimension. Figure 1 (codes grouped by dimensions) illustrates that the feature combination on the SINGLE model is ill-suited for the Process codes, and half the Dual Process and Substance codes. Recall for each code for the SINGLE model are mostly below or at par with the recall for each code in the MULTIPLE model. Thus, creating a one-size-fits-all initial model may not be optimal when training data is limited. Figure 2 (codes sorted based on gold frequency as shown beside the code names in the x-axis) exhibits that the SINGLE model is able to achieve similar recall to the MULTIPLE model for codes with over 100 positive examples in the training data. Precision for these codes are also higher compared to codes with sparse positive examples. This finding is promising because it implies that creating a one-size-fits-all initial ML model may be possible even for a multidimensional coding scheme if there are more than 100 positive examples for each code.

## 4 Conclusion and Future Work

We conclude that creating an optimal initial one-size-fits-all ML model for all codes in a multi-dimensional coding scheme using only a single feature combination is not possible when codes with sparse positive examples are present, and training data is limited, which may be common in real world content analysis projects in social science research. However, our findings also show that the potential of using a one-size-fits-all model increases when the size of positive examples for each code in the gold standard corpus are above 100. For social scientists who may not possess the technical skills needed for feature selection to optimize the initial ML model, this discovery confirms that we can create a "canned" model using a single combination of features that would work well in text classification for a wide range of codes with the condition that researchers must be able to provide sufficient positive examples above a certain threshold to train the initial model. This would make the application of machine learning for qualitative content analysis more accessible to social scientists.

The initial ML model with low precision means that the model is over-predicting. As a result, human annotators will have to correct more false positives in the machine annotations. For future work, we plan to experiment with different sampling strategies to pick the most "profitable" machine annotations to be corrected by human annotators. We will also work on designing an interactive and adaptive user interface to promote greater understanding of machine learning outputs for our target users.

## Acknowledgments

This material is based upon work supported by the National Science Foundation under Grant No. IIS-1111107. Kevin Crowston is supported by the National Science Foundation. Any opinions, findings, and conclusions or recommendations expressed in this material are those of the author(s) and do not necessarily reflect the views of the National Science Foundation. The authors wish to thank Janet Marsden for assisting with the feature testing experiments, and gratefully acknowledge helpful suggestions by the reviewers.

## References

Broadwell, G. A., Stromer-Galley, J., Strzalkowski, T., Shaikh, S., Taylor, S., Liu, T., Boz, U., Elia, A., Jiao, L., Webb, N. (2013). Modeling Sociocultural phenomena in discourse. *Natural Language Engineering*, *19*(02), 213–257.

Crowston, K., Allen, E. E., & Heckman, R. (2012). Using natural language processing technology for qualitative data analysis. *International Journal of Social Research Methodology*, *15*(6), 523–543.

Dönmez, P., Rosé, C., Stegmann, K., Weinberger, A., & Fischer, F. (2005). Supporting CSCL with automatic corpus analysis technology. In *Proceedings of 2005 Conference on Computer Support for Collaborative Learning* (pp. 125–134).

Evans, M., McIntosh, W., Lin, J., & Cates, C. (2007). Recounting the courts? Applying automated content analysis to enhance empirical legal research. *Journal of Empirical Legal Studies*, *4*(4), 1007–1039.

Evans, W. (1996). Computer-supported content analysis: Trends, tools, and techniques. *Social Science Computer Review*, *14*(3), 269–279.

Grimmer, J., & Stewart, B. M. (2013). Text as data: The promise and pitfalls of automatic content analysis methods for political texts. *Political Analysis*, *21*(3), 267–297.

Ishita, E., Oard, D. W., Fleischmann, K. R., Cheng, A.-S., & Templeton, T. C. (2010). Investigating multi-label classification for human values. *Proceedings of the American Society for Information Science and Technology*, *47*(1), 1–4.

Liew, J. S. Y., McCracken, N., & Crowston, K. (2014). Semi-automatic content analysis of qualitative data. In *iConference 2014 Proceedings* (pp. 1128–1132).

Miles, M. B., & Huberman, A. M. (1994). *Qualitative data analysis: An expanded sourcebook* (2nd ed.). Sage.

Misiolek, N., Crowston, K., & Seymour, J. (2012). Team dynamics in long-standing technology-supported virtual teams. Presented at the Academy of Management Annual Meeting, Organizational Behavior Division, Boston, MA.

Zhu, H., Kraut, R. E., Wang, Y.-C., & Kittur, A. (2011). Identifying shared leadership in Wikipedia. In *Proceedings of the SIGCHI Conference on Human Factors in Computing Systems* (pp. 3431–3434). New York, NY, USA.

# Power of Confidence:
# How Poll Scores Impact Topic Dynamics in Political Debates

**Vinodkumar Prabhakaran**
Dept. of Computer Science
Columbia University
New York, NY
vinod@cs.columbia.edu

**Ashima Arora**
Dept. of Computer Science
Columbia University
New York, NY
aa3470@columbia.edu

**Owen Rambow**
CCLS
Columbia University
New York, NY
rambow@ccls.columbia.edu

## Abstract

In this paper, we investigate how topic dynamics during the course of an interaction correlate with the power differences between its participants. We perform this study on the US presidential debates and show that a candidate's power, modeled after their poll scores, affects how often he/she attempts to shift topics and whether he/she succeeds. We ensure the validity of topic shifts by confirming, through a simple but effective method, that the turns that shift topics provide substantive topical content to the interaction. A paper describing this work is published in the ACL 2014 Joint Workshop on Social Dynamics and Personal Attributes in Social Media.



*Proceedings of the ACL 2014 Workshop on Language Technologies and Computational Social Science*, page 49,
Baltimore, Maryland, USA, June 26, 2014. 

# Predicting Fine-grained Social Roles with Selectional Preferences

**Charley Beller** charleybeller@jhu.edu
**Craig Harman** craig@craigharman.net
**Benjamin Van Durme** vandurme@cs.jhu.edu
Human Language Technology Center of Excellence
Johns Hopkins University, Baltimore, MD USA

## Abstract

Selectional preferences, the tendencies of predicates to select for certain semantic classes of arguments, have been successfully applied to a number of tasks in computational linguistics including word sense disambiguation, semantic role labeling, relation extraction, and textual inference. Here we leverage the information encoded in selectional preferences to the task of predicting fine-grained categories of authors on the social media platform Twitter. First person uses of verbs that select for a given social role as subject (e.g. *I teach* ... for **teacher**) are used to quickly build up binary classifiers for that role.

## 1 Introduction

It has long been recognized that linguistic predicates preferentially select arguments that meet certain semantic criteria (Katz and Fodor, 1963; Chomsky, 1965). The verb *eat* for example selects for an animate subject and a comestible object. While the information encoded by selectional preferences can and has been used to support natural language processing tasks such as word sense disambiguation (Resnik, 1997), syntactic disambiguation (Li and Abe, 1998) and semantic role labeling (Gildea and Jurafsky, 2002), much of the work on the topic revolves around developing methods to induce selectional preferences from data. In this setting, end-tasks can be used for evaluation of the resulting collection. Ritter et al. (2010) gave a recent overview of this work, breaking it down into class-based approaches (Resnik, 1996; Li and Abe, 1998; Clark and Weir, 2002; Pantel et al., 2007), similarity-based approaches (Dagan et al., 1999; Erk, 2007), and approaches using discriminative (Bergsma et al., 2008) or generative probabilistic models (Rooth et al., 1999) like their own.

One of our contributions here is to show that the literature on selectional preferences relates to the analysis of the first person content transmitted through social media. We make use of a "quick and dirty" method for inducing selectional preferences and apply the resulting collections to the task of predicting fine-grained latent *author attributes* on Twitter. Our method for inducing selectional preferences is most similar to class-based approaches, though unlike approaches such as by Resnik (1996) we do not require a WordNet-like ontology.

The vast quantity of informal, first-person text data made available by the rise of social media platforms has encouraged researchers to develop models that predict broad user categories like age, gender, and political preference (Garera and Yarowsky, 2009; Rao et al., 2010; Burger et al., 2011; Van Durme, 2012b; Zamal et al., 2012). Such information is useful for large scale demographic research that can fuel computational social science advertising.

Similarly to Beller et al. (2014), we are interested in classification that is finer-grained than gender or political affiliation, seeking instead to predict *social roles* like *smoker*, *student*, and *artist*. We make use of a light-weight, unsupervised method to identify selectional preferences and use the resulting information to rapidly bootstrap classification models.

## 2 Inducing Selectional Preferences

Consider the task of predicting social roles in more detail: For a given role, e.g. **artist**, we want a way to distinguish role-bearing from non-role-bearing users. We can view each social role as being a fine-grained version of a semantic class of the sort required by class-based approaches to selectional preferences (e.g. the work by Resnik (1996) and those reviewed by Light and Greiff (2002)). The goal then is to identify a set of verbs that preferen-



*Proceedings of the ACL 2014 Workshop on Language Technologies and Computational Social Science*, pages 50–55,
Baltimore, Maryland, USA, June 26, 2014. ©2014 Association for Computational Linguistics

tially select that particular class as argument. Once we have a set of verbs for a given role, simple pattern matches against first person subject templates like *I* ___ can be used to identify authors that bear that social role.

In order to identify verbs that select for a given role $r$ as subject we use an unsupervised method inspired by Bergsma and Van Durme (2013) that extracts features from third-person content (i.e. newswire) to build classifiers on first-person content (i.e. tweets). For example, if we read in a news article that *an artist drew ...*, we can take a tweet saying *I drew ...* as potential evidence that the author bears the **artist** social role.

We first count all verbs $v$ that appear with role $r$ as subject in the web-scale, part-of-speech tagged n-gram corpus, Google V2 (Lin et al., 2010). The resulting collection of verbs is then ranked by computing their pointwise mutual information (Church and Hanks, 1990) with the subject role $r$. The PMI of a given role $r$ and a verb $v$ that takes $r$ as subject is given as:

$$\mathrm{PMI}(r,v) = \log \frac{P(r,v)}{P(r)P(v)}$$

Probabilities are estimated from counts of the role-verb pairs along with counts matching the generic subject patterns *he* ___ and *she* ___ which serve as general background cases. This gives us a set of verbs that preferentially select for the subset of persons filling the given role.

The output of the PMI ranking is a high-recall list of verbs that preferentially select the given social role as subject over a background population. Each such list then underwent a manual filtering step to rapidly remove non-discriminative verbs and corpus artifacts. One such artifact from our corpus was the term *wannabe* which was spuriously elevated in the PMI ranking based on the relative frequency of the bigram *artist wannabe* as compared to *she wannabe*. Note that in the first case *wannabe* is best analyzed as a noun, while in the second case a verbal analysis is more plausible. The filtering was performed by one of the authors and generally took less than two minutes per list. The rapidity of the filtering step is in line with findings such as by Jacoby et al. (1979) that relevance based filtering involves less cognitive effort than generation. After filtering the lists contained fewer than 40 verbs selecting each social role.

In part because of the pivot from third- to first-person text we performed a precision test on the remaining verbs to identify which of them are likely to be useful in classifying twitter users. For each remaining verb we extracted all tweets that contained the first person subject pattern *I* ___ from a small corpus of tweets drawn from the free public 1% sample of the Twitter Firehose over a single month in 2013. Verbs that had no matches which appeared to be composed by a member of the associated social role were discarded. Using this smaller high-precision set of verbs, we collected tweets from a much larger corpus drawn from 1% sample over the period 2011-2013.

One notable feature of the written English in social media is that sentence subjects can be optionally omitted. Subject-drop is a recognized feature of other informal spoken and written registers of English, particularly 'diary dialects' (Thrasher, 1977; Napoli, 1982; Haegeman and Ihsane, 2001; Weir, 2012; Haegeman, 2013; Scott, 2013). Because of the prevalence of subjectless cases we collected two sets of tweets: those matching the first person subject pattern *I* ___ and those where the verb was tweet initial. Example tweets for each of our social roles can be seen in Table 2.

## 3 Classification via selectional preferences

We conducted a set of experiments to gauge the strength of the selectional preference indicators for each social role. For each experiment we used balanced datasets for training and testing with half of the users taken from a random background sample and half from a collection of users identified as belonging to the social role. Base accuracy was thus 50%.

To curate the collections of positively identified users we crowdsourced a manual verification procedure. We use the popular crowdsourcing platform Mechanical Turk[1] to judge whether, for a tweet containing a given verb, the author held the role that verb prefers as subject. Each tweet was judged using 5-way redundancy.

Mechanical Turk judges ("Turkers") were presented with a tweet and the prompt: *Based on this tweet, would you think this person is a* ARTIST*?* along with four response options: *Yes*, *Maybe*, *Hard to tell*, and *No*. An example is shown in Figure 1.

We piloted this labeling task with a goal of 20 tweets per verb over a variety of social roles.

[1] https://www.mturk.com/mturk/

| | |
|---|---|
| **Artist** | |
| *draw* | Yeaa this a be the first time I draw my shit onn |
| **Athlete** | |
| *play* | @[user] @[user] i have got the night off tonight because I played last night and I am going out for dinner so won't be able to come" |
| **Blogger** | |
| *blogged* | @[user] I decided not to renew. I blogged about it on the fan club. a bit shocked no neg comments back to me |
| **Cheerleader** | |
| *cheer* | I really dont wanna cheer for this game I have soo much to do |
| **Christian** | |
| *thank* | Had my bday yesterday 3011 nd had a good night with my friends. I thank God 4 His blessings in my life nd praise Him 4 adding another year. |
| **DJ** | |
| *spin* | Quick cut session before I spin tonight |
| **Filmmaker** | |
| *film* | @[user] apparently there was no audio on the volleyball game I filmed so...there will be no "NAT sound" cause I have no audio at all |
| **Media Host** | |
| *interview* | Oh. I interviewed her on the @[user] . You should listen to the interview. Its awesome! @[user] @[user] @[user] |
| **Performer** | |
| *perform* | I perform the flute... kareem shocked... |
| **Producer** | |
| *produce* | RT @[user]: Wow 2 films in Urbanworld this year-1 I produced ... [URL] |
| **Smoker** | |
| *smoke* | I smoke , i drank .. was my shit bra ! |
| **Stoner** | |
| *puff* | I'm a cigarello fiend smokin weed like its oxygen Puff pass, nigga I puff grass till I pass out |
| **Student** | |
| *finish* | I finish school in March and my friend birthday in March ... |
| **Teacher** | |
| *teach* | @[user] home schooled I really wanna find out wat it's like n making new friends but home schooling is cool I teach myself mums ill |

Table 1: Example verbs and sample tweets collected using them in the first person subject pattern (*I* ___).

Each answer was associated with a score (Yes = 1, Maybe = .5, Hard to tell = No = 0) and aggregated across the five judges, leading to a range of possible scores from 0.0 to 5.0 per tweet. We found in development that an aggregate score of 4.0 led to an acceptable agreement rate between the Turkers and the experimenters, when the tweets were randomly sampled and judged internally.

Verbs were discarded for being either insufficiently accurate or insufficiently prevalent in the corpus. From the remaining verbs, we identified users with tweets scoring 4.0 or better as the positive examples of the associated social roles. These positively identified user's tweets were scraped using the Twitter API in order to construct user-specific corpora of positive examples for each role.

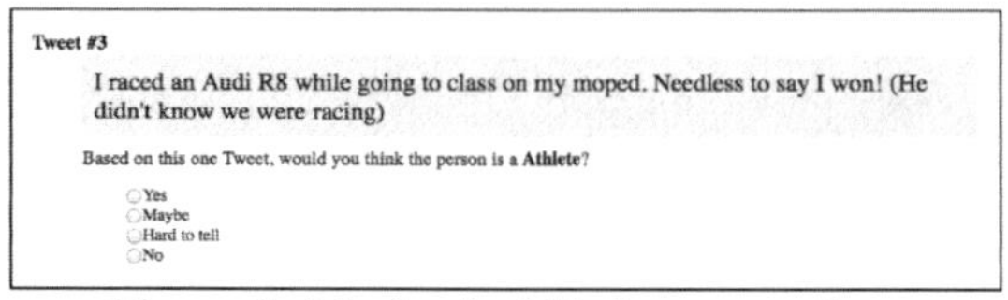


Figure 1: Mechanical Turk presentation

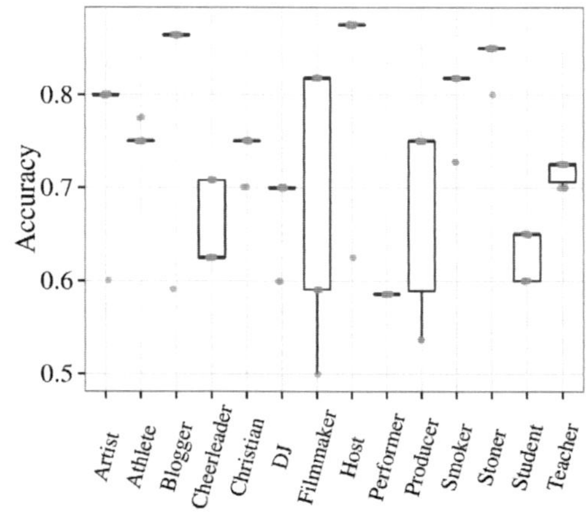


Figure 2: Accuracy of classifier trained and tested on balanced set contrasting agreed upon Twitter users of a given role, against users pulled at random from the 1% stream.

### 3.1 General Classification

The positively annotated examples were balanced with data from a background set of Twitter users to produce training and test sets. These test sets were usually of size 40 (20 positive, 20 background), with a few classes being sparser (the smallest test set had only 28 instances). We used the `Jerboa` (Van Durme, 2012a) platform to convert our data to binary feature vectors over a unigram vocabulary filtered such that the minimum frequency was 5 (across unique users). Training and testing was done with a log-linear model via `LibLinear` (Fan et al., 2008). Results are shown in Figure 2. As can be seen, a variety of classes in this balanced setup can be predicted with accuracies in the range of 80%. This shows that the information encoded in selectional preferences contains discriminating signal for a variety of these social roles.

### 3.2 Conditional Classification

How accurately can we predict membership in a given class when a Twitter user sends a tweet matching one of the collected verbs? For example, if one sends a tweet saying *I race* ..., then how likely is it that the author is an **athlete**?

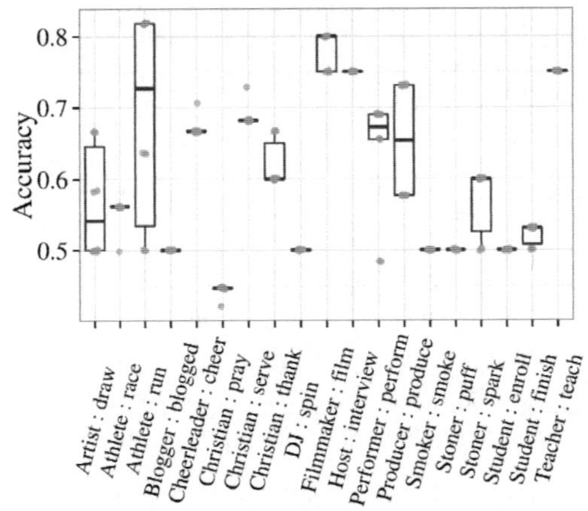


Figure 3: Results of positive vs negative by verb. Given that a user writes a tweet containing *I interview ...* or *Interviewing ...* we are about 75% accurate in identifying whether or not the user is a Radio/Podcast Host.

| # Users | # labeled | # Pos | # Neg | Attribute |
|---|---|---|---|---|
| 199022 | 516 | 63 | 238 | Artist-draw |
| 45162 | 566 | 40 | 284 | Athlete-race |
| 1074289 | 1000 | 54 | 731 | Athlete-run |
| 9960 | 15 | 14 | 0 | Blogger-blog |
| 2204 | 140 | 57 | 18 | College Student-enroll |
| 247231 | 1000 | 85 | 564 | College Student-finish |
| 60486 | 845 | 61 | 524 | Cheerleader-cheer |
| 448738 | 561 | 133 | 95 | Christian-pray |
| 92223 | 286 | 59 | 180 | Christian-serve |
| 428337 | 307 | 78 | 135 | Christian-thank |
| 17408 | 246 | 17 | 151 | DJ-spin |
| 153793 | 621 | 53 | 332 | Filmmaker-film |
| 36991 | 554 | 42 | 223 | Radio Host-interview |
| 43997 | 297 | 81 | 97 | Performer-perform |
| 69463 | 315 | 71 | 100 | Producer-produce |
| 513096 | 144 | 74 | 8 | Smoker-smoke |
| 5542 | 124 | 49 | 15 | Stoner-puff |
| 5526 | 229 | 59 | 51 | Stoner-spark |
| 149244 | 495 | 133 | 208 | Teacher-teach |

Table 2: Numbers of positively and negatively identified users by indicative verb.

Using the same collection as the previous experiment, we trained classifiers conditioned on a given verb term. Positive instances were taken to be those with a score of 4.0 or higher, with negative instances taken to be those with scores of 1.0 or lower (strong agreement by judges that the original tweet did not provide evidence of the given role). Classification results are shown in figure 3. Note that for a number of verb terms these thresholds left very sparse collections of users. There were only 8 users, for example, that tweeted the phrase *I smoke ...* but were labeled as negative instances of Smokers. Counts are given in Table 2.

Despite the sparsity of some of these classes, many of the features learned by our classifiers make intuitive sense. Highlights of the most highly weighted unigrams from the classification

| Verb | Feature (_Rank) |
|---|---|
| **draw** | drawing, art, book$_4$, sketch$_{14}$, paper$_{19}$ |
| **race** | race, hard, winter, won$_{11}$, training$_{16}$, run$_{17}$ |
| **run** | awesome, nike$_6$, fast$_9$, marathon$_{20}$ |
| **blog** | notes, boom, hacked$_4$, perspective$_9$ |
| **cheer** | cheer, pictures, omg, text, literally |
| **pray** | through, jesus$_3$, prayers$_7$, lord$_{14}$, thank$_{17}$ |
| **serve** | lord, jesus, church, blessed, pray, grace |
| **thank** | [ ], blessed, lord, trust$_{11}$, pray$_{12}$ |
| **enroll** | fall, fat, carry, job, spend, fail$_{15}$ |
| **finish** | hey, wrong, may$_8$, move$_9$, officially$_{14}$ |
| **spin** | show, dj, music, dude, ladies, posted, listen |
| **film** | please, wow, youtube, send, music$_8$ |
| **perform** | [ ], stuck, act, song, tickets$_7$, support$_{16}$ |
| **produce** | follow, videos$_8$, listen$_{10}$, single$_{11}$, studio$_{13}$, |
| **interview** | fan, latest, awesome, seems |
| **smoke** | weakness, runs, ti, simply |
| **puff** | bout, $7, smh$_9$, weed$_{10}$ |
| **spark** | dont, fat$_5$, blunt$_6$, smoke$_{11}$ |
| **teach** | forward, amazing, students, great, teacher$_7$ |

Table 3: Most-highly indicative features that a user holds the associated role given that they used the phrase *I VERB* along with select features within the top 20.

experiments are shown in Table 3. Taken together these features suggest that several of our roles can be distinguished from the background population by focussing on typical language use. The use of terms like, e.g., *sketch* by artists, *training* by athletes, *jesus* by Chrisitians, and *students* by teachers conforms to expected pattern of language use.

## 4 Conclusion

We have shown that verb-argument selectional preferences relates to the content-based classification strategy for latent author attributes. In particular, we have presented initial studies showing that mining selectional preferences from third-person content, such as newswire, can be used to inform latent author attribute prediction based on first-person content, such as that appearing in social media services like Twitter.

Future work should consider the question of *priors*. Our study here relied on balanced class experiments, but the more fine-grained the social role, the smaller the subset of the population we might expect will possess that role. Estimating these priors is thus an important point for future work, especially if we wish to couple such demographic predictions within a larger automatic system, such as the aggregate prediction of targeted sentiment (Jiang et al., 2011).

**Acknowledgements** This material is partially based on research sponsored by the NSF under grant IIS-1249516 and by DARPA under agreement number FA8750-13-2-0017 (DEFT).

## References


Charley Beller, Rebecca Knowles, Craig Harman, Shane Bergsma, Margaret Mitchell, and Benjamin Van Durme. 2014. I'm a belieber: Social roles via self-identification and conceptual attributes. In *Proceedings of the 52nd Annual Meeting of the Association for Computational Linguistics*.

Shane Bergsma and Benjamin Van Durme. 2013. Using Conceptual Class Attributes to Characterize Social Media Users. In *Proceedings of ACL*.

Shane Bergsma, Dekang Lin, and Randy Goebel. 2008. Discriminative learning of selectional preference from unlabeled text. In *Proceedings of the Conference on Empirical Methods in Natural Language Processing*, pages 59–68. Association for Computational Linguistics.

John D. Burger, John Henderson, George Kim, and Guido Zarrella. 2011. Discriminating gender on Twitter. In *Proceedings of EMNLP*.

Noam Chomsky. 1965. *Aspects of the Theory of Syntax*. Number 11. MIT press.

Kenneth Ward Church and Patrick Hanks. 1990. Word association norms, mutual information, and lexicography. *Computational linguistics*, 16(1):22–29.

Stephen Clark and David Weir. 2002. Class-based probability estimation using a semantic hierarchy. *Computational Linguistics*, 28(2).

Ido Dagan, Lillian Lee, and Fernando CN Pereira. 1999. Similarity-based models of word cooccurrence probabilities. *Machine Learning*, 34(1-3):43–69.

Katrin Erk. 2007. A simple, similarity-based model for selectional preferences. In *Proceeding of the 45th Annual Meeting of the Association for Computational Linguistics*, volume 45, page 216.

Rong-En Fan, Kai-Wei Chang, Cho-Jui Hsief, Xiang-Rui Wang, and Chih-Jen Lin. 2008. Liblinear: A library for large linear classification. *Journal of Machine Learning Research*, (9).

Nikesh Garera and David Yarowsky. 2009. Modeling latent biographic attributes in conversational genres. In *Proceedings of ACL*.

Daniel Gildea and Daniel Jurafsky. 2002. Automatic labeling of semantic roles. *Computational linguistics*, 28(3):245–288.

Liliane Haegeman and Tabea Ihsane. 2001. Adult null subjects in the non-pro-drop languages: Two diary dialects. *Language acquisition*, 9(4):329–346.

Liliane Haegeman. 2013. The syntax of registers: Diary subject omission and the privilege of the root. *Lingua*, 130:88–110.

Larry L Jacoby, Fergus IM Craik, and Ian Begg. 1979. Effects of decision difficulty on recognition and recall. *Journal of Verbal Learning and Verbal Behavior*, 18(5):585–600.

Long Jiang, Mo Yu, Xiaohua Liu, and Tiejun Zhao. 2011. Target-dependent twitter sentiment classification. In *Proceedings of ACL*.

Jerrold J Katz and Jerry A Fodor. 1963. The structure of a semantic theory. *language*, pages 170–210.

Hang Li and Naoki Abe. 1998. Generalizing case frames using a thesaurus and the MDL principle. *Computational linguistics*, 24(2):217–244.

Marc Light and Warren Greiff. 2002. Statistical models for the induction and use of selectional preferences. *Cognitive Science*, 26(3):269–281.

Dekang Lin, Kenneth Church, Heng Ji, Satoshi Sekine, David Yarowsky, Shane Bergsma, Kailash Patil, Emily Pitler, Rachel Lathbury, Vikram Rao, Kapil Dalwani, and Sushant Narsale. 2010. New tools for web-scale n-grams. In *Proc. LREC*, pages 2221–2227.

Donna Jo Napoli. 1982. Initial material deletion in English. *Glossa*, 16(1):5–111.

Patrick Pantel, Rahul Bhagat, Bonaventura Coppola, Timothy Chklovski, and Eduard H Hovy. 2007. ISP: Learning inferential selectional preferences. In *HLT-NAACL*, pages 564–571.

Delip Rao, David Yarowsky, Abhishek Shreevats, and Manaswi Gupta. 2010. Classifying latent user attributes in Twitter. In *Proceedings of the Workshop on Search and Mining User-generated Contents (SMUC)*.

Philip Resnik. 1996. Selectional constraints: An information-theoretic model and its computational realization. *Cognition*, 61(1):127–159.

Philip Resnik. 1997. Selectional preference and sense disambiguation. In *Proceedings of the ACL SIGLEX Workshop on Tagging Text with Lexical Semantics: Why, What, and How*, pages 52–57. Washington, DC.

Alan Ritter, Masaum, and Oren Etzioni. 2010. A latent dirichlet allocation method for selectional preferences. In *Proceedings of the 48th Annual Meeting of the Association for Computational Linguistics*, pages 424–434. Association for Computational Linguistics.

Mats Rooth, Stefan Riezler, Detlef Prescher, Glenn Carroll, and Franz Beil. 1999. Inducing a semantically annotated lexicon via EM-based clustering. In *Proceedings of the 37th annual meeting of the Association for Computational Linguistics*, pages 104–111. Association for Computational Linguistics.

Kate Scott. 2013. Pragmatically motivated null subjects in English: A relevance theory perspective. *Journal of Pragmatics*, 53:68–83.

Randolph Thrasher. 1977. One way to say more by saying less: A study of so-called subjectless sentences. *Kwansei Gakuin University Monograph Series*, 11.

Benjamin Van Durme. 2012a. Jerboa: A toolkit for randomized and streaming algorithms. Technical Report 7, Human Language Technology Center of Excellence, Johns Hopkins University.

Benjamin Van Durme. 2012b. Streaming analysis of discourse participants. In *Proceedings of EMNLP*.

Andrew Weir. 2012. Left-edge deletion in English and subject omission in diaries. *English Language and Linguistics*, 16(01):105–129.

Faiyaz Al Zamal, Wendy Liu, and Derek Ruths. 2012. Homophily and latent attribute inference: Inferring latent attributes of Twitter users from neighbors. In *Proceedings of ICWSM*.

# Predicting Party Affiliations from European Parliament Debates

**Bjørn Høyland**
Department of Political Science
University of Oslo
bjorn.hoyland@stv.uio.no

**Jean-François Godbout**
Department of Political Science
University of Montreal
godboutj@umontreal.ca

**Emanuele Lapponi**
Department of Informatics
University of Oslo
emanuel@ifi.uio.no

**Erik Velldal**
Department of Informatics
University of Oslo
erikve@ifi.uio.no

## Abstract

This paper documents an ongoing effort to assess whether party group affiliation of participants in European Parliament debates can be automatically predicted on the basis of the content of their speeches, using a support vector machine multi-class model. The work represents a joint effort between researchers within Political Science and Language Technology.

## 1 Introduction

The European Parliament (EP) is the directly elected parliamentary institution of the European Union (EU), elected once every five years by voters from across all 28 member states. An important arena for the political activity in the EP is the plenary sittings, the forum where all (currently 766) elected members of the European Parliament (MEPs) from all member states participate in plenary debates (in all represented languages, simultaneously translated). Our current work investigates to what extent the party affiliation of the legislators in the plenary debates can be predicted on the basis of their speeches. More specifically, the goal is to predict the party affiliation of plenary speakers in the $6^{th}$ European Parliament (July 2004 – July 2009) on the basis of the party affiliations of plenary speakers in the $5^{th}$ European Parliament (July 1999 – July 2004).[1] One premise for the success of such an approach is that differences in ideology and belief systems are reflected in differences in choice of words in plenary debates. Another premise is that a shared belief system translates to the same choice of party group. As discussed below, systematic differences in prediction performance in the data can be used to reveal interesting differences in the extent to which these premises hold for various subgroups of MEPs. While this is further discussed in Section 4, we first describe the data sets in some more detail in Section 2 and present some preliminary results in Section 3.

[1]The data have been collected from the official website of the European Parliament, where verbatim reports from each plenary sitting are published:
www.europarl.europa.eu/plenary/en/debates.html

## 2 Data sets and experimental set-up

The debates from the $5^{th}$ EP are used for training an SVM(Cortes and Vapnik, 1995) multi-class classifier[2] which we then apply for predicting party affiliations in the $6^{th}$ EP. We do 5-fold cross validation experiments on the $5^{th}$ term for model tuning. Data points in the model correspond to speakers; participants in the debates in the EP labeled with their political party. All recorded speeches for a given speaker are conflated in a single vector. Although we can so far only report results for models using fairly basic feature types – various bag-of-words configurations based on lemmas, stems or full word-forms – combined with more linguistically informed ones,

[2]We use the freely available $\text{SVM}^{multiclass}$ toolkit, implementing the multi-class formulation of support vector machines described by Crammer and Singer (2001) with very fast optimization for linear kernels based on the algorithm for estimating Structural SVMs described by Tsochantaridis et al. (2004). For more information see; www.cs.cornell.edu/people/tj/svm_light/svm_multiclass.html



*Proceedings of the ACL 2014 Workshop on Language Technologies and Computational Social Science*, pages 56–60,
Baltimore, Maryland, USA, June 26, 2014. 

| Party | MEPs |
|---|---|
| PSE | 211 |
| EPP-ED | 272 |
| ELDR | 65 |
| GUE/NGL | 48 |
| V/ALE | 55 |
| UEN | 38 |
| Total | 689 |

Table 1: Distribution of members across the various political parties in the training data from the $5^{th}$ European Parliament plenary debates.

like part-of-speech (PoS) tags and dependency relations; work is already in progress with respect to assessing the usefulness of e.g. class-based features drawn from unsupervised word clustering and modeling semantic phenomena such as negation, speculation and sentiment. Large-scale experimentation with different features sets and hyperparameters is made possible by running experiments on a large high-performance computing (HPC) cluster.

The main political groups in the European Parliament during these terms were the Christian Democratic / Conservative (EPP-ED), the Social-Democratic (PES), the Liberal (ELDR), the Green (V/ALE), the Socialists (GUE/NGL), and Right (UEN). Note that experiments only focus on the six largest political parties, excluding the smaller and more marginal ones which are often more unstable or ad-hoc configurations, including independent MEPs with various forms of Anti-EU ideologies. To give an idea of class distribution, the number of MEPs for all parties in our training set is listed in Table 1. Our $5^{th}$ EP term training set comprises a total of 689 MEPs while our $6^{th}$ term test set comprises 818. It is worth pointing out that in the $6^{th}$ EP, roughly 75% of the data corresponds to MEPs from the old member states while 25% test are MEPs from the new member states. Of the members from the old member states, roughly 53% of the MEPs are incumbents while the remainders are freshmen (we return to this property in Section 4 below).

In order to facilitate reproducibility of reported results and foster further research, all data sets are available for download, including party labels and all (automatic) linguistic annotations. [3]

| | Baseline | stem | dep/stem |
|---|---|---|---|
| Acc | 0.394 | 0.476 | 0.492 |
| Prec | 0.065 | 0.439 | 0.458 |
| Rec | 0.166 | 0.399 | 0.393 |
| $F_1$ | 0.094 | 0.418 | 0.423 |

Table 3: Results of the 5-fold cross-validation experiments on the training data for the majority-class baseline, a model trained on stems and one enriched with dependency-disambiguated stems.

## 3 Preliminary results

In addition to reporting results for the SVM classifier, we also include figures for a simple majority-class baseline approach, i.e., simply assigning all MEPs in the test set to the largest political party, EPP-ED. For evaluating the various approaches we will be reporting precision (Prec), recall (Rec) and $F_1$ for each individual class/party, in addition to the corresponding macro-averaged scores across all parties. Note that for one-of classification problems like the one we are dealing with here, micro-averaging would simply correspond to accuracy (with Prec = Rec = $F_1$, since the number of false positives and false negatives would be the same). While we also report accuracy, it is worth bearing in mind that accuracy will overemphasize performance on the large classes when working with skewed class distributions like we do here.

In order to study the effects of different surface features and classifier-tuning, we conduct a number of 5-fold cross-validation experiments on the training data using different feature combinations, for each empirically determining the best value for the C-parameter (i.e., the regularization parameter of the SVM classifier, governing the trade-off between training error and margin size). In this initial experiments we trained different models with various configurations of non-normalized tokens (i.e., observed word forms), stems, lemmas and PoS- and dependency-disambiguated tokens and stems. The best performing configuration so far turns out to be the dependency disambiguated stems with the observed optimal C-value of 0.8, with $F_1$ over two percentage points higher than the model trained on stems alone at the same C-

[3]Downloadable at `http://emanuel.at.ifi.uio.no/debates_data.tar.gz`

| | PSE | EPP-ED | ELDR | GUE/NGL | V/ALE | UEN | total |
|---|---|---|---|---|---|---|---|
| PSE | 111 | 36 | 15 | 9 | 6 | 1 | 178 |
| EPP-ED | 123 | 286 | 77 | 13 | 12 | 31 | 542 |
| ELDR | 3 | 3 | 7 | 0 | 1 | 0 | 14 |
| GUE/NGL | 2 | 0 | 1 | 18 | 1 | 0 | 22 |
| V/ALE | 3 | 2 | 2 | 5 | 25 | 1 | 38 |
| UEN | 7 | 9 | 3 | 1 | 8 | 4 | 32 |
| total | 249 | 336 | 105 | 46 | 53 | 37 | 826 |
| Acc | 0.445 | 0.851 | 0.066 | 0.391 | 0.471 | 0.108 | **0.551** |
| Prec | 0.623 | 0.527 | 0.500 | 0.818 | 0.657 | 0.166 | **0.549** |
| Rec | 0.445 | 0.851 | 0.066 | 0.391 | 0.555 | 0.108 | **0.403** |
| $F_1$ | 0.519 | 0.651 | 0.117 | 0.529 | 0.602 | 0.131 | **0.464** |

Table 2: Confusion matrix showing predicted (horizontal) and true (vertical) party affiliations, together with accuracy, precision, recall and $F_1$ scores for system predictions. Overall accuracy and macro-averaged precision, recall and $F_1$ (presented in bold text) can be compared to majority-class baseline results of Acc=0.410, Prec=0.068, Rec=0.166 and $F_1$=0.097.

value point (see Table 3 for details). This indicates that linguistically informed features do provide the model with relevant information.

Results obtained by applying the best-performing configuration from our development experiments to the test data are presented in Table 2, together with a confusion matrix for the classifier assignments. Party-wise $F_1$ and accuracy scores in addition to overall accuracy and macro-averaged precision, recall and $F_1$ are shown in the bottom four rows; compare values in bold text to majority-class baseline results of Acc=0.407, Prec=0.069, Rec=0.166 and $F_1$=0.097. There are two groups with comparatively poor prediction scores, the Liberal (ELDR) and the Right (UEN). In the case of the former, there are two key factors that may account for this: (1) Ideological compositions of the group and, (2) coalition-formation in the EP. Firstly, ELDR consists of delegations from national parties that tend to locate themselves between the Social-Democratic (PES) and the Christian-Democratic / Conservative parties (EPP-ED) at the national arena. Due to differences in the ideological landscape across EU member states, some members of the ELDR may find themselves holding views that are closer to those held by PES or EPP-ED than ELDR representatives from some countries. Secondly, in the period under investigation, ELDR tended to form coalitions with the EPP-ED on some policy areas and with the PES on others. As MEPs mainly speak on policies related to the Committees they serve on, misclassifications as PES or EPP-ED may be a reflection of the coaltion-formation on the committees they served on (Hix and Høyland, 2013). When it comes to UEN, misclassification as EPP-ED may be explained in terms of shared ideology. In some cases, the membership of UEN rather than EPP-ED is due to historical events rather than ideological considerations (McElroy and Benoit, 2012).

## 4 Research questions

This section briefly outlines some of the questions we will be focusing on in the ongoing work of analyzing the predictions of the SVM classifier in more detail. In most cases this analysis will consist of comparing prediction performance across various relevant subsets of MEPs while looking for systematic differences.

**Contribution of linguistic features** Much of the work done to date in "text-as-data" approaches in social sciences has been based on relatively simple and surface oriented features, typically bag-of-words models, perhaps combined with term weighting and stemming for word normalization (for an overview of what is currently considered best practice, see Grimmer and Stewart (2013)). Much of the methodology can be seen as imports from the fields of information retrieval and data mining rather than natural language processing.

A relevant question for the current work is the extent to which more linguistically informed features can contribute to the task of predicting political affiliation, compared to "surface features" based solely on directly observable lexical information. One of our goals is to asses whether more accurate models can be built by including richer feature sets with more linguistically informed features, like part-of-speech (PoS) tags, dependency relations, class-based features drawn from unsupervised word clustering, negation scope analysis, and more. The preliminary results already demonstrates that linguistically motivated features can be useful for the current task, but there are still many more feature types and combinations to be explored.

**Differences between new and old member states** Ten countries joined the European Union in 2004. This offered a rare opportunity for the existing party groups to substantively increase their share of the seats in the European Parliament by recruiting national party delegations from the new member states. As most of the new member states have a relative short history of competitive multiparty system, there were weaker ties between parties in new and old member states when compared to previous rounds of enlargement. Since the allocation of office spoils in the EP is fairly proportional among party groups it was assumed that national parties from the new member states – less ideologically committed to any of the belief systems held by the traditional Western European party families – would shift the allocation of some offices in the EP by opting to join certain party group who controlled a larger share of ministerial portfolios. If there are large differences in classifier performance between members from new and old members states, this can provide support for the hypothesis that national party delegations from new member states joined the existing party groups for other reasons than simply shared ideological beliefs and goals. Høyland and Godbout (2008) presented similar preliminary results that already hint at this tendency. The ongoing collaboration will further explore this question by targeting it in new ways.

**Differences between incumbents and freshmen MEPs** This point is tightly connected to the previous. Given that our training and testing data are correspond to distinct consecutive terms of parliament, one should determine whether any differences in prediction performance for MEPs from new and old member states can be explained simply by the fact that the latter will include many MEPs that appear both in the training and the test data (i.e., speakers participating in the debates in both the $5^{th}$ and $6^{th}$ term). In order to factor out any such "incumbency effect", we will also investigate whether any differences can be found in prediction performance between incumbents and "freshmen" (members who joined the EP after the 2004 elections) originating from old member states only.

**Differences between political domains** Another effect we would like to measure is whether there are any systematic differences in prediction performance across different political topics or domains. Among other things this could indicate that the language use is more politicized or ideologically charged in debates concerning certain political issues. Much of the work in the European Parliament is carried out in specialized committees that prepare reports that will later be debated and voted on in the plenary. By coupling the debates with information about which legislative standing committee has handled each particular case, we would be able to automatically break down our results according to political domain. This could be achieved using a resource like that described by Høyland et al. (2009). Examples of committee domains include Foreign Affairs, International Trade, Legal Affairs, Regional Development, Economic and Monetary Affairs, and Internal Market and Consumer Protection, to name a few. Another possibility here would be to train separate specialized classifiers for debates falling within the domain of each specialized committee directly.

## 5 Summary

This paper has outlined an interdisciplinary effort to explore whether the recorded speeches from the plenary debates of the European Parliament can be utilized by an SVM classifier to correctly predict the party affiliations of the participants. Preliminary experimental results already demonstrates that such predictions can indeed be made – also demonstrating the contribution of linguistically informed features – and the paper has outlined a number of related research questions currently being pursued in ongoing work.

## References


[Cortes and Vapnik1995] Corinna Cortes and Vladimir Vapnik. 1995. Support-vector networks. *Machine Learning*, 20(3):273–297, September.

[Crammer and Singer2001] Koby Crammer and Yoram Singer. 2001. On the algorithmic implementation of multiclass kernel-based vector machines. *Journal of Machine Learning Research*, 2:265–292, December.

[Grimmer and Stewart2013] Justin Grimmer and Brandon M. Stewart. 2013. Text as data: The promise and pitfalls of automatic content analysis methods for political texts. *Political Analysis*, 21(3):267–297.

[Hix and Høyland2013] Simon Hix and Bjørn Høyland. 2013. The empowerment of the european parliament. *Annual Review of Political Science*, 16:171–189.

[Høyland and Godbout2008] Bjørn Høyland and Jean-François Godbout. 2008. Lost in translation? predicting party group affiliation from european parliament debates. In *On-line Proceedings of the Fourth Pan-European Conference on EU Politics*.

[Høyland et al.2009] Bjørn Høyland, Indraneel Sircar, and Simon Hix. 2009. Forum section: an automated database of the european parliament. *European Union Politics*, 10(1):143–152.

[McElroy and Benoit2012] Gail McElroy and Kenneth Benoit. 2012. Policy positioning in the european parliament. *European Union Politics*, 13(1):150–167.

[Tsochantaridis et al.2004] Ioannis Tsochantaridis, Thomas Hofmann, Thorsten Joachims, and Yasemin Altun. 2004. Support vector machine learning for interdependent and structured output spaces. In *Proceedings of the 21st International Conference on Machine Learning*.

# Temporal Analysis of Language through Neural Language Models

**Yoon Kim**[*] **Yi-I Chiu**[*] **Kentaro Hanaki**[*] **Darshan Hegde**[*] **Slav Petrov**[◇]

[*]New York University, New York
[◇]Google Inc., New York

{yhk255, yic211, kh1615, dh1806}@nyu.edu
slav@google.com

## Abstract

We provide a method for automatically detecting change in language across time through a chronologically trained neural language model. We train the model on the Google Books Ngram corpus to obtain word vector representations specific to each year, and identify words that have changed significantly from 1900 to 2009. The model identifies words such as *cell* and *gay* as having changed during that time period. The model simultaneously identifies the specific years during which such words underwent change.

## 1 Introduction

Language changes across time. Existing words adopt additional senses (*gay*), new words are created (*internet*), and some words 'die out' (many irregular verbs, such as *burnt*, are being replaced by their regularized counterparts (Lieberman et al., 2007)). Traditionally, scarcity of digitized historical corpora has prevented applications of contemporary machine learning algorithms—which typically require large amounts of data—in such temporal analyses. Publication of the Google Books Ngram corpus in 2009, however, has contributed to an increased interest in *culturomics*, wherein researchers analyze changes in human culture through digitized texts (Michel et al., 2011).

Developing computational methods for detecting and quantifying change in language is of interest to theoretical linguists as well as NLP researchers working with diachronic corpora. Methods employed in previous work have been varied, from analyses of word frequencies to more involved techniques (Guolordava et al. (2011); Mihalcea and Nataste (2012)). In our framework, we train a Neural Language Model (NLM) on yearly corpora to obtain word vectors for each year from 1900 to 2009. We chronologically train the model by initializing word vectors for subsequent years with the word vectors obtained from previous years.

We compare the cosine similarity of the word vectors for same words in different years to identify words that have moved significantly in the vector space during that time period. Our model identifies words such as *cell* and *gay* as having changed between 1900–2009. The model additionally identifies words whose change is more subtle. We also analyze the yearly movement of words across the vector space to identify the specific periods during which they changed. The trained word vectors are publicly available.[1]

## 2 Related Work

Previously, researchers have computationally investigated diachronic language change in various ways. Mihalcea and Nastase (2012) take a supervised learning approach and predict the time period to which a word belongs given its surrounding context. Sagi et al. (2009) use a variation of Latent Semantic Analysis to identify semantic change of specific words from early to modern English. Wijaya and Yeniterzi (2011) utilize a Topics-over-Time model and K-means clustering to identify periods during which selected words move from one topic/cluster to another. They correlate their findings with the underlying historical events during that time. Gulordava and Baroni (2011) use co-occurrence counts of words from 1960s and 1990s to detect semantic change. They find that the words identified by the model are consistent with evaluations from human raters. Popescu and Strapparava (2013) employ statistical tests on frequencies of political, social, and emotional words to identify and characterize epochs.

Our work contributes to the domain in sev-

[1]http://www.yoon.io



*Proceedings of the ACL 2014 Workshop on Language Technologies and Computational Social Science*, pages 61–65,
Baltimore, Maryland, USA, June 26, 2014. 

eral ways. Whereas previous work has generally involved researchers manually identifying words that have changed (with the exception of Gulordava and Baroni (2011)), we are able to automatically identify them. We are additionally able to capture a word's yearly movement and identify periods of rapid change. In contrast to previous work, we simultaneously identify words that have changed and also the specific periods during which they changed.

## 3 Neural Language Models

Similar to traditional language models, NLMs involve predicting a set of future word given some history of previous words. In NLMs however, words are projected from a sparse, 1-of-V encoding (where V is the size of the vocabulary) onto a lower dimensional vector space via a hidden layer. This allows for better representation of semantic properties of words compared to traditional language models (wherein words are represented as indices in a vocabulary set). Thus, words that are semantically close to one another would have word vectors that are likewise 'close' (as measured by a distance metric) in the vector space. In fact, Mikolov et al. (2013a) report that word vectors obtained through NLMs capture much deeper level of semantic information than had been previously thought. For example, if $x_w$ is the word vector for word $w$, they note that $x_{apple} - x_{apples} \approx x_{car} - x_{cars} \approx x_{family} - x_{families}$. That is, the concept of pluralization is learned by the vector representations (see Mikolov et al. (2013a) for more examples).

NLMs are but one of many methods to obtain word vectors—other techniques include Latent Semantic Analysis (LSA) (Deerwester et al., 1990), Latent Dirichlet Allocation (LDA) (Blei et al., 2003), and variations thereof. And even within NLMs there exist various architectures for learning word vectors (Bengio et al. (2003); Mikolov et al. (2010); Collobert et al. (2011); Yih et al. (2011)). We utilize an architecture introduced by Mikolov et al. (2013b), called the Skip-gram, which allows for efficient estimation of word vectors from large corpora.

In a Skip-gram model, each word in the corpus is used to predict a window of surrounding words (Figure 1). To ensure that words closer to the current word are given more weight in training, distant words are sampled less frequently.[2] Training is done through stochastic gradient descent and backpropagation. The word representations are found in the hidden layer. Despite its simplicity—and thus, computational efficiency—compared to other NLMs, Mikolov et al. (2013b) note that the Skip-gram is competitive with other vector space models in the Semantic-Syntactic Word Relationship test set when trained on the same data.

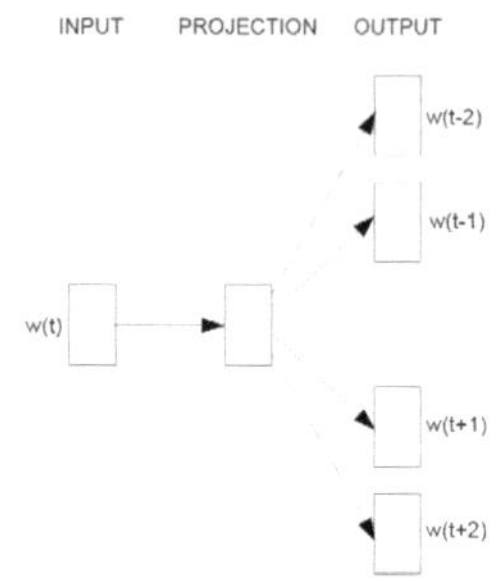


Figure 1: Architecture of a Skip-gram model (Mikolov et al., 2013b).

### 3.1 Training

The Google Books Ngram corpus contains Ngrams from approximately 8 million books, or 6% of all books published (Lin et al., 2012). We sample 10 million 5-grams from the English fiction corpus for every year from 1850–2009. We lower-case all words after sampling and restrict the vocabulary to words that occurred at least 10 times in the 1850–2009 corpus.

For the model, we use a window size of 4 and dimensionality of 200 for the word vectors. Within each year, we iterate over epochs until convergence, where the measure of convergence is defined as the average angular change in word vectors between epochs. That is, if $V(y)$ is the vocabulary set for year $y$, and $x_w(y,e)$ is the word vector for word $w$ in year $y$ and epoch number $e$, we continue iterating over epochs until,

$$\frac{1}{|V(y)|} \sum_{w \in V(y)} \arccos \frac{x_w(y,e) \cdot x_w(y,e-1)}{\|x_w(y,e)\| \|x_w(y,e-1)\|}$$

is below some threshold. The learning rate is set to 0.01 at the start of each epoch and linearly decreased to 0.0001.

[2]Specifically, given a maximum window size of $W$, a random integer $R$ is picked from range $[1, W]$ for each training word. The current training word is used to predict $R$ previous and $R$ future words.

| Most Changed | | Least Changed | |
|---|---|---|---|
| Word | Similarity | Word | Similarity |
| *checked* | 0.3831 | *by* | 0.9331 |
| *check* | 0.4073 | *than* | 0.9327 |
| *gay* | 0.4079 | *for* | 0.9313 |
| *actually* | 0.4086 | *more* | 0.9274 |
| *supposed* | 0.4232 | *other* | 0.9272 |
| *guess* | 0.4233 | *an* | 0.9268 |
| *cell* | 0.4413 | *own* | 0.9259 |
| *headed* | 0.4453 | *with* | 0.9257 |
| *ass* | 0.4549 | *down* | 0.9252 |
| *mail* | 0.4573 | *very* | 0.9239 |

Table 1: Top 10 most/least changed words from 1900–2009, based on cosine similarity of words in 2009 against their 1900 counterparts. Infrequent words (words that occurred less than 500 times) are omitted.

Once the word vectors for year $y$ have converged, we initialize the word vectors for year $y+1$ with the previous year's word vectors and train on the $y + 1$ data until convergence. We repeat this process for 1850–2009. Using an open source implementation in the `gensim` package, training took approximately 4 days on a 2.9 GHz machine.

## 4 Results and Discussion

For the analysis, we treat 1850–1899 as an initialization period and begin our study from 1900.

### 4.1 Word Comparisons

By comparing the cosine similarity between same words across different time periods, we are able to detect words whose usage has changed. We are also able to identify words that did not change. Table 1 has a list of 10 most/least changed words between 1900 and 2009. We note that almost all of the least changed words are function words. For the changed words, many of the identified words agree with intuition (e.g. *gay*, *cell*, *ass*). Others are not so obvious (e.g. *checked*, *headed*, *actually*). To better understand how these words have changed, we look at the composition of their neighboring words for 1900 and 2009 (Table 2).

As a further check, we search Google Books for sentences that contain the above words. Below are some example sentences from 1900 and 2009 with the word *checked*:

1900: "However, he *checked* himself in time, saying —"

1900: "She was about to say something further, but she *checked* herself."

2009: "He'd *checked* his facts on a notepad from his back pocket."

2009: "I *checked* out the house before I let them go inside."

| Word | Neighboring Words in 1900 | Neighboring Words in 2009 |
|---|---|---|
| *gay* | *cheerful*<br>*pleasant*<br>*brilliant* | *lesbian*<br>*bisexual*<br>*lesbians* |
| *cell* | *closet*<br>*dungeon*<br>*tent* | *phone*<br>*cordless*<br>*cellular* |
| *checked* | *checking*<br>*recollecting*<br>*straightened* | *checking*<br>*consulted*<br>*check* |
| *headed* | *haired*<br>*faced*<br>*skinned* | *heading*<br>*sprinted*<br>*marched* |
| *actually* | *evidently*<br>*accidentally*<br>*already* | *really*<br>*obviously*<br>*nonetheless* |

Table 2: Top 3 neighboring words (based on cosine similarity) specific to each time period for the words identified as having changed.

At the risk of oversimplifying, the resulting sentences indicate that in the past, *checked* was more frequently used with the meaning *"to hold in restraint"*, whereas now, it is more frequently used with the meaning *"to verify by consulting an authority"* or *"to inspect so as to determine accuracy"*. Given that *check* is a highly polysemous word, this seems to be a case in which the popularity of a word's sense changed over time.

Conducting a similar exercise for *actually*, we obtain the following sentences:

1900: "But if ever he *actually* came into property, she must recognize the change in his position."

1900: "Whenever a young gentleman was not *actually* engaged with his knife and fork or spoon —"

2009: "I can't believe he *actually* did that!"

2009: "Our date was *actually* one of the most fun and creative ones I had in years."

Like the above, this seems to be a case in which the popularity of a word's sense changed over time (from *"to refer to what is true or real"* to *"to express wonder or surprise"*).

### 4.2 Periods of Change

As we chronologically train the model year-by-year, we can plot the time series of a word's distance to its neighboring words (from different years) to detect periods of change. Figure 2 (above) has such a plot for the word *cell* compared to its early neighbors, *closet* and *dungeon*, and the more recent neighbors, *phone* and *cordless*. Figure 2 (below) has a similar plot for *gay*.

Such plots allow us to identify a word's period of change relative to its neighboring words,

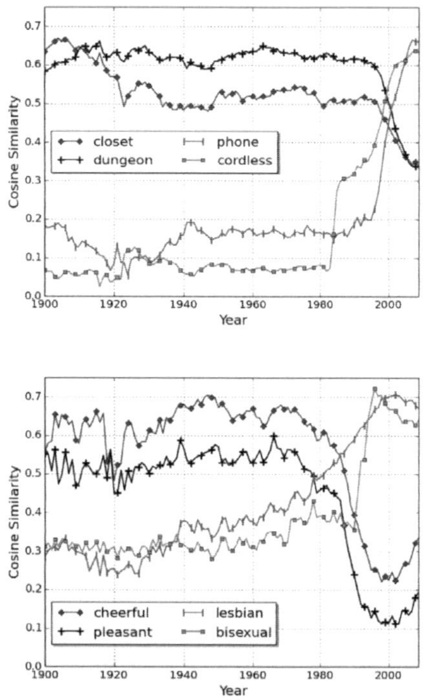


Figure 2: (Above) Time trend of the cosine similarity between *cell* and its neighboring words in 1900 (*closet, dungeon*) and 2009 (*phone, cordless*). (Below) Similar plot of *gay* and its neighboring words in 1900 (*cheerful, pleasant*) and 2009 (*lesbian, bisexual*).

and thus provide context as to how it evolved. This may be of use to researchers interested in understanding (say) when *gay* started being used as a synonym for *homosexual*. We can also identify periods of change independent of neighboring words by analyzing the cosine similarity of a word against itself from a reference year (Figure 3). As some of the change is due to sampling and random drift, we additionally plot the average cosine similarity of all words against their reference points in Figure 3. This allows us to detect whether a word's change during a given period is greater (or less) than would be expected from chance. We note that for *cell*, the identified period of change (1985–2009) coincides with the introduction—and subsequent adoption—of the cell phone by the general public.[3] Likewise, the period of change for *gay* agrees with the gay movement which began around the 1970s (Wijaya and Yeniterzi, 2011).

### 4.3 Limitations

In the present work, identification of a changed word is conditioned on its occurring often enough

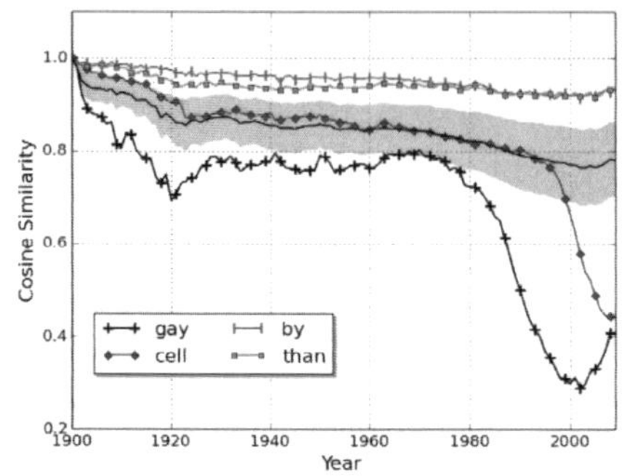


Figure 3: Plot of the cosine similarity of changed (*gay, cell*) and unchanged (*by, than*) words against their 1900 starting points. Middle line is the average cosine similarity of all words against their starting points in 1900. Shaded region corresponds to one standard deviation of errors.

in the study period. If a word's usage decreased dramatically (or stopped being used altogether), its word vector will have remained the same and hence it will not show up as having changed. One way to overcome this may be to combine the cosine distance and the frequency to define a new metric that measures how a word's usage has changed.

## 5 Conclusions and Future Work

In this paper we provided a method for analyzing change in the written language across time through word vectors obtained from a chronologically trained neural language model. Extending previous work, we are able to not only automatically identify words that have changed but also the periods during which they changed. While we have not extensively looked for connections between periods identified by the model and real historical events, they are nevertheless apparent.

An interesting direction of research could involve analysis and characterization of the different types of change. With a few exceptions, we have been deliberately general in our analysis by saying that a word's *usage* has changed. We have avoided inferring the *type* of change (e.g. semantic vs syntactic, broadening vs narrowing, pejoration vs amelioration). It may be the case that words that undergo (say) a broadening in senses exhibit regularities in how they move about the vector space, allowing researchers to characterize the type of change that occurred.

[3] http://library.thinkquest.org/04oct/02001/origin.htm

## References


Y. Bengio, R. Ducharme, P. Vincent. 2003. Neural Probabilitistic Language Model. *Journal of Machine Learning Research 3:1137–1155.*

D. Blei, A. Ng, M. Jordan, J. Lafferty. 2003. Latent Dirichlet Allocation. *Journal of Machine Learning Research 3:993–1022.*

R. Collobert, J. Weston, L. Bottou, M. Karlen, K. Kavukcuglu, P. Kuksa. 2011. Natural Language Processing (Almost) from Scratch. *Journal of Machine Learning Research 12:2493–2537.*

S. Deerwester, S. Dumais, G. Furnas, T. Landauer, R. Harshman. 2011. Indexing by Latent Semantic Analysis. *Journal of the American Society for Information Science, 41(6):391–407.*

K. Gulordava, M. Baroni. 2011. A Distributional Similarity Approach to the Detection of Semantic Change in the Google Books Ngram Corpus. *Proceedings of the GEMS 2011 Workshop.*

E. Lieberman, J.B. Michel, J. Jackson, T. Tang, M.A. Nowak. 2007. Quantifying the evolutionary dynamics of language. *Nature, 449: 716–716, October.*

Y. Lin, J.B. Michel, E.L. Aiden, J. Orwant, W. Brockman, S. Petrov. 2012. Syntactic Annotations for the Google Books Ngram Corpus. *Proceedings of the Association for Computational Linguistics 2012.*

J.B Michel, Y.K. Shen, A.P. Aiden, A. Veres, M.K. Gray, J.P. Pickett, D. Hoiberg, D. Clancy, P. Norvig, J. Orwant, S.Pinker, M.A. Nowak, E.L. Aiden. 2011. Quantitative Analysis of Culture Using Millions of Digitized Books. *Science, 331(6014): 176–182, January.*

R. Mihalcea, V. Nastase. 2012. Word Epoch Disambiguation: Finding How Words Change Over Time. *Proceedings of the Association for Computational Linguistics 2012.*

T. Mikolov, M. Karafiat, L. Burget, J. Cernocky, S. Khudanpur. 2010. Recurrent Neural Network Based Language Model. *Proceedings of Interspeech.*

T. Mikolov, W.T Yih, G. Zweig. 2013a. Linguistic Regularities in Continuous Space Word Representations. *Proceedings of NAACL-HLT 2013, 746–751.*

T. Mikolov, K. Chen, G. Corrado, J.Dean. 2013b. Efficient Estimation of Word Representations in Vector Space *arXiv Preprint.*

O. Popescu, C. Strapparava. 2013. Behind the Times: Detecting Epoch Changes using Large Corpora. *International Joint Conference on Natural Language Processing, 347–355*

E. Sagi, S. Kaufmann, B. Clark 2009. Semantic Density Analysis: Comparing Word Meaning across Time and Phonetic Space. *Proceedings of the EACL 2009 Workshop on GEMS: 104–111.*

D.T. Wijaya, R. Yeniterzi. 2011. Understanding semantic change of words over centuries. *Proceedings of the 2011 international workshop on DEtecting and Exploiting Cultural diversiTy on the social web: 35–40.*

W. Yih, K. Toutanova, J. Platt, C. Meek. 2011. Learning Discriminative Projections for Text Similarity Measures. *Proceedings of the Fifteenth Conference on Computational Natural Language Learning, 247–256.*

# Using Simple NLP Tools to Trace the Globalization of the Art World

**Alix Rule**
Dept. of Sociology
Columbia University
New York, NY, USA
aer2132@columbia.edu

**Zhongyu Wang** and **Rupayan Basu**
Dept. of Computer Science
Columbia University
New York, NY, USA
{zw2259, rb3034}@columbia.edu

**Mohamed AlTantawy**
Agolo, Inc.
New York, NY, USA
mohamed@agolo.com

**Owen Rambow**
Center for Computational Learning Systems
Columbia University
New York, NY, USA
rambow@ccls.columbia.edu

## Abstract

We introduce a novel task, that of associating relative time with cities in text. We show that the task can be performed using NLP tools and techniques. The task is deployed on a large corpus of data to study a specific phenomenon, namely the temporal dimension of contemporary arts globalization over the first decade of the 21st century.

## 1 Introduction

This paper reports on the use of fairly simple Natural Language Processing (NLP) technology as a tool for social research. We seek to understand the globalization of contemporary art, relying on releases for art events worldwide over the period of 1999-2012. A first phase of the project exploited Named-Entity Recognition (NER) to extract cities named in the corpus.

In this second phase of the research, we turn our attention to a novel task: the temporal dimension captured in these texts. By identifying the timing of geographically-cited events, we are able to examine how the history and projected future of the art world evolve alongside, and as a result of, its current geographical structure. To determine whether cities named in press releases refer to events that occur in the past, the present, or the future, we need methods for resolving time expressed in text relative to the time of the release of the text. We use the Stanford Temporal TaggerSUTime (Chang and Manning, 2012), as well as rules we have built on top of the Stanford part-of-speech tagger (Toutanova et al., 2003), to identify the temporal referent of each city mentioned. The two systems in combination perform slightly better than either does alone, and at a high enough level of accuracy to produce meaningful data for network analysis. We start by describing the project in more detail in Section 2, as well as the data we use in Section 3. Section 4 discusses our method for identifying the temporal location of named events. The networks we build using this data afford some preliminary insights into the dynamics of contemporary arts globalization, which we present in Section 5. Our aim here is not, however, to offer definitive conclusions about change in the art world. Rather, we present these analyses as proof of concept to demonstrate how a novel NLP task can help advance a particular agenda in social research.

## 2 The Goals of the Project

The shifting geography of contemporary art is of interest to social scientists as an instance of cultural globalization (Bourdieu, 1999; Crane, 2008). Scholars and contemporary art practitioners alike have remarked on changes in the geography of globally-significant art activity in recent decades (Vanderlinden and Filipovic, 2005; McAndrew, 2008; Quemin, 2006). Accounts of these dynamics often converge: for example, many have pointed to the role that speculation in the art of the developing world plays in fragmenting the once geographically-concentrated field of contemporary art (e.g., (Lee, 2012; Stallabrass, 2006)). Such claims remain largely a matter of conjecture, however, having never been subjected to systematic empirical scrutiny.

Because of the difficulties of compiling appropriate data, contemporary arts globalization has rarely been studied using quantitative methods. The few quantitative analyses that exist focus on particular cities (Velthius, 2013), individual artists (Buchholz, forthcoming), or a particular category



*Proceedings of the ACL 2014 Workshop on Language Technologies and Computational Social Science*, pages 66–70,
Baltimore, Maryland, USA, June 26, 2014. 

of art-related events, for example fairs (Quemin, 2013). Our project relies on NLP techniques to solve the problems of data collection that have limited previous research endeavors. We extract information from a large and growing corpus of press releases for contemporary art events occurring worldwide. An initial phase of the project revealed for the first time an object that has resisted empirical description: the contemporary global art world. The research was able to track changes in the art worlds geographic structure over the period of 2001 until 2012. Named Entity Recognition (NER) was used to identify cities mentioned in the body text of announcements as the location of other significant contemporary art events. Pooling documents over a given time window yielded a dynamic network of cities, enabling the researchers to track the evolution of the art world. The analysis revealed that a distinct central core of cities all in Europe and North America enjoyed a remarkably stable ranking as top art locales over the period; however, as the art world expanded, connection to these capitals became less important as an entry to the art world for locations outside the global north (Rule and Brandt, 2013).

"The city that I believed was my past, is my future, my present; the years I have spent in Europe are an illusion, I always was (and will be) in Buenos Aires" (Borges, 1978). Borges' remarks capture a paradox about places of significance: important places are places where important things *have happened* and *will happen*–but this is so from the viewpoint of the present, which is always evolving. This insight implies that in order to understand the dynamics shaping the geography of significant art activity, analysts need to disentangle the real time in which attributions of significance to locations occur, from the relative timing of the events that make them significant. The current phase of our research attempts to assess how the geographical evolution of the art world shapes contemporary arts history and its projected future. It does so by considering how events mentioned in the corpus are located in time, relative to the event in question. We build upon the NER-based strategy developed in Phase 1 for identifying cities as the location of important events. Here, however, we distinguish cities as the location of events in the past, present, or future.

> [The artist] has exhibited extensively in group shows and biennials across Europe, Asia and the Americas including Manifesta 8, the Third Moscow Biennale and Sharjah Biennial. His work is the subject of a major monograph, Laurent Grasso: The Black-Body Radiation (Les Presses du Reel, 2009). As the 2008 Laureate of the Marcel Duchamp Prize, Grasso presented a special exhibition at the Centre Georges Pompidou (2009). Grassos work is currently on view at La Maison Rouge in Paris in an exhibition of the Olbricht Collection; forthcoming are solo exhibitions at the Galerie nationale du Jeu de Paume, Paris in 2012 and at the Musée d'art contemporain de Montréal, Canada in 2013.

Figure 1: A sample press release

## 3 Data

We draw on corpus of press releases for contemporary art events worldwide, distributed over the premier email digest service for contemporary art. The digest serves a professional clientele, and sends out 3-5 press releases a day. These emails are free to the digest's 90,000 subscribers (compare to *Artforum*'s circulation of 35,000). Press releases are both written and paid for by the institutions sponsoring the events they announce. The corpus covers the years 1999 to 2012; it contains 10,566 documents and 6362284. Our automated detection, checked by human annotators, identified 1007 unique cities.

We conceive of each press release as an attempt to raise the status of the event in question by mentioning other high-status events to which it is related. Pooling the references of cities across documents thus gives rise to a network, analogous to a citation network. The press releases are rather conventionalized, and name cities almost exclusively as the location of important related events. The format is not just used by this particular digest service, but is common to the art world generally. A sample is shown in Figure 1.

## 4 Time Identification

Cities associated with art events are identified using an NER-based approach, which performs at an f-measure of 64.5 and which we do not further describe in this paper. We use *two* approaches for temporal resolution to assess whether the cities mentioned are the locations of events that happened in the past, are currently happening, or expected to happen in the future.

The first approach analyzes explicit time ex-

| | Accuracy | Past | | | Current | | | Future | | |
|---|---|---|---|---|---|---|---|---|---|---|
| | | *P* | *R* | *F1* | *P* | *R* | *F1* | *P* | *R* | *F1* |
| Baseline* | 63.8 | 0 | 0 | 0 | 63.8 | 100 | 77.9 | 0 | 0 | 0 |
| Lexical (L) | 66.6 | **79.3** | 56.6 | 66.1 | 75.3 | 75.5 | 75.4 | 21.6 | 36.5 | 27.1 |
| Grammaticized (G) | 73.4 | 70.0 | 48.8 | 57.5 | 74.9 | **89.0** | 81.4 | 64.5 | 38.5 | **48.2** |
| $L_G$ | 69.2 | 77.2 | 73.6 | **75.4** | 81.2 | 71.8 | 76.2 | 23.2 | **42.3** | 29.9 |
| $G_L$ | 74.0 | 71.0 | 51.2 | 59.5 | 75.5 | 89.0 | 81.7 | 64.5 | 38.5 | **48.2** |
| $L_G$ & $G_L$ | **78.0** | 70.5 | **76.0** | 73.1 | **82.2** | 85.6 | **83.9** | **65.5** | 36.5 | 46.9 |

Table 1: Accuracy and precision, recall and F-measure for past, current and future events. *Baseline: Tagging all events as *current*.

pressions in dates, time durations, holidays, etc. The second approach uses verbal tense to resolve grammaticized reference to time. In both approaches: (1) We use distance within a sentence as a heuristic to associate a temporal expression to a city. (2) Cities associated with art events are tagged as *past*, *current* or *future*, where ***current*** is the default tag. This section describes both approaches and how they can be combined to enhance the performance.

### 4.1 Explicit Lexical Temporal Expressions

Explicit temporal expressions could be partial or complete dates (*Jan-01*, *March 2nd, 2014*), specific named days (*Christmas 2001*), deictic time expressions (*last Wednesday*), time durations (*the past five years*), seasons (*next fall*), etc.

We use the Stanford Temporal Tagger, SUTime (Chang and Manning, 2012) to detect and evaluate Temporal expressions relative to the publication date of the press release. Temporal expressions that evaluate to incomplete dates take on the missing date components from the publication date. If the temporal expression resolves to a date before, same as or after the publication date, then the event associated with the city is tagged as past, current, or future event respectively. Cities that are not associated with explicit temporal expressions are given the default tag: *current*.

### 4.2 Grammaticized Temporal Expressions

Tense is grammaticalization of location in time (Comrie, 1985). Our tense-based approach has two steps. First, the Stanford part-of-speech tagger (Toutanova et al., 2003) is used to identify the POS tags of all tokens in the documents. Second, we use hand-written rules to identify the temporal interpretation of every event. The rules are mostly based on the POS tags of verbs; we use the tag sets from the Penn Treebank Project (Marcus et al., 1993). We use only the verbal tags: VB (*Verb, base form*), VBD (*Verb, past tense*), VBG (*Verb, gerund or present participle*), *etc.* and MD (*Modal*). Here are some examples of the rules; events associated with: (1) VBP or VBZ are tagged as *current*. (2) VBD are tagged as *past*. (3) VB that are preceded by will/MD are tagged as *future*.

### 4.3 Results and Combining of the Two Approaches

During development, we found that the two time tagging approaches perform well in different situations. For example, the lexical approach has the higher recall (66.1%) for past event as writers often mention the exact date of past events. However, in the case of current events dates are seldom mentioned, the present tense is enough to communicate that the event mentioned in a sentence is ongoing. This accounts for the higher recall of the grammaticized (89%) as against the lexical approach (75.5%) for current events. If we do not assign *current* by default to the failed cases in both the lexical and grammaticized approaches, the recall for current events drops drastically for the lexical approach (75.5% $\searrow$ 0.69%) compared to the grammaticized approaches (89% $\searrow$ 81.5%).

Combining the two approaches improves the performance of the time tagging task. We start with one approach to tag an event and when that approach fails (does not provide an answer), the other approach kicks in. If both approaches fail, the event is tagged by default as *current*. For example, in approach Grammaticized$_{Lexical}$ ($G_L$), when the Grammaticized approach fails to tag an event, the Lexical approach is used. The best combination is achieved by running the Lexical$_{Grammaticized}$ ($L_G$) first; if the output tag is *past*, accept its answer; otherwise run the Grammaticized$_{Lexical}$ system ($G_L$) and accept its verdict. If $G_L$ has no answer, choose *present*. The accuracy of this approach is 78.0%. For more details, see table 1. Please note that analyses in section 5 rely on the Grammaticized$_{Lexical}$ ($G_L$) approach.

| | | 2001-04 | 2005-08 | 2009-12 |
|---|---|---|---|---|
| # Documents | | 1063 | 3352 | 4687 |
| Past | Nodes | 238 | 600 | 645 |
| | Edges | 6477 | 34901 | 51213 |
| | Share | 21.5% | 25.8% | 31.3% |
| Curr. | Nodes | 509 | 957 | 995 |
| | Edges | 37087 | 152279 | 186928 |
| | Share | 70.3% | 63.8% | 49.8% |
| Fut. | Nodes | 158 | 352 | 460 |
| | Edges | 2047 | 11270 | 16851 |
| | Share | 8.2% | 10.4% | 14.0% |

Table 2: Properties of networks of past, present, and future art events, for three periods. "Share" refers to the percentage of events in relative time during a given period.

## 5 Creation and Interpretation of Networks

To analyze the geography of the art world, we generated networks of events in relative time over three four-year periods: 2001-2004; 2005-2008; and 2009-2012. Nodes represent cities named as the location of art events, and edges co-citations from a particular geographical and temporal standpoint. Specifically, we attribute ties between cities of the past, present or future of a given period when they are mentioned together in press releases for events currently occurring in the same city. Ties are weighted to reflect the number of co-mentions. For example, if Basel is noted twice as a future event location by press releases for events in New York, and LA is mentioned by New York press releases three times, the edge between Basel and LA receives an edge weight of 2, reflecting the number of shared mentions.

Basic properties of the nine resulting networks are displayed in table 2. Notice the marked difference in the distribution of events in relative time between 2005-2008 and 2009-2012. Cities mentioned in connection with events in both the future and the past figure as a greater proportion of the total in the last, as compared to the middle period. Though we consider the possibility that this is an artifact of the data, it seems more to likely that the shift reflects the impact of a real world development: namely, the global economic recession, which began in 2008 and had profound effect on funding for contemporary art. In the context of the economic contraction, it seems that both contemporary arts future and its history become more important relative to its present.

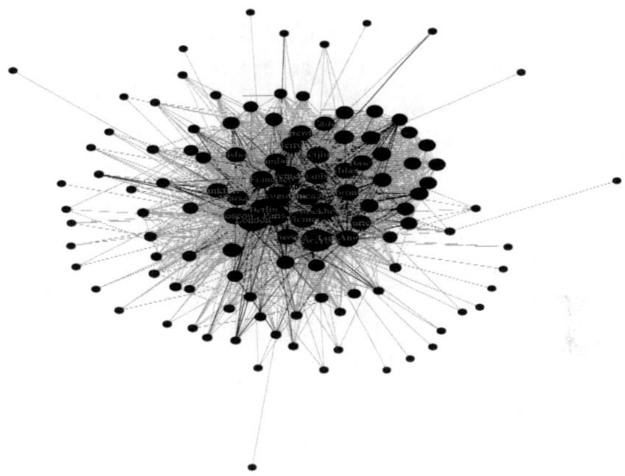

Figure 2: Future of the global contemporary art world, 2009-2012

Figure 2 shows the network of future events arising from 2009-2012. Recall that the graph captures the world's future, as it is structured by the geography of significant art world activity during this period. Just as in Borges remarks about Buenos Aires, we observe here how important places in the art worlds present shape the map of its future.

This graph suggests an art world that is rather conservative, more so, at least, than accounts of the speculation driving its globalization would imply. The network exhibits a classic core-periphery structure; the cities at its center are the "big" art capitals of the global north: London, New York, Berlin, Paris, Venice. In other words, the common proposition that the "hype" around emerging art markets has de-centered the contemporary art world is not borne out by a close empirical examination from the perspective of the hype-generators themselves. Rather, it would seems that the role of these cities as the prime location for contemporary art in the present enables them to project themselves as the location of significant art activity in the future.

## References


Jorge Luis Borges. 1978. *Obra Poetica 1923-1976*. Emece.

P. Bourdieu. 1999. The social conditions of the international circulation of ideas. pages 220–228.

Angel X Chang and Christopher Manning. 2012. Sutime: A library for recognizing and normalizing time expressions. In *LREC*, pages 3735–3740.

Bernard Comrie. 1985. *Tense*, volume 17. Cambridge University Press.

Diana Crane. 2008. Globalization and cultural flows/networks. *The Sage handbook of cultural analysis*, pages 359–381.

Pamela M Lee. 2012. *Forgetting the Art World*. MIT Press.

Mitchell P Marcus, Mary Ann Marcinkiewicz, and Beatrice Santorini. 1993. Building a large annotated corpus of english: The penn treebank. *Computational linguistics*, 19(2):313–330.

Clare McAndrew. 2008. *The International Art Market: A Survey of Europe in a Global Context*. European Fine Art Foundation (TEFAF).

Alain Quemin. 2006. Globalization and mixing in the visual arts an empirical survey of high cultureand globalization. *International sociology*, 21(4):522–550.

Alain Quemin. 2013. International contemporary art fairs in a globalizedart market. *European Societies*, 15(2):162–177.

Alix Rule and Philipp Brandt. 2013. Dynamic art objects: The evolving structural composition of the global art scene. Citation Networks Section of the SUNBELT International Social Networks Research Association Conference.

Julian Stallabrass. 2006. *Contemporary art: a very short introduction*. Oxford University Press.

Kristina Toutanova, Dan Klein, Christopher D Manning, and Yoram Singer. 2003. Feature-rich part-of-speech tagging with a cyclic dependency network. In *HLT-NAACL - Volume 1*, pages 173–180.

Barbara Vanderlinden and Elena Filipovic. 2005. *The Manifesta decade: debates on contemporary art exhibitions and biennials in post-wall Europe*. The MIT Press.

Mordechai Edgar Velthius. 2013. The art market in new york, basel and tokyo: Deconstructing the economics of aesthetic consumption. *Art and Money*.

# Issue Framing as a Generalizable Phenomenon

**Amber Boydstun**
University of California at Davis

## Abstract

Framing—portraying an issue from one perspective to the necessary exclusion of alternative perspectives—is a central concept in political communication. It is also a powerful political tool, as evidenced through experiments and single-issue studies beyond the lab. Yet compared to its significance, we know very little about framing as a generalizable phenomenon. Do framing dynamics, such as the evolution of one frame into another, play out the same way for all issues? Under what conditions does framing influence public opinion and policy? Understanding the general patterns of framing dynamics and effects is thus hugely important. It is also a serious challenge, thanks to the volume of text data, the dynamic nature of language, and variance in applicable frames across issues (e.g., the 'innocence' frame of the death penalty debate is irrelevant for discussing smoking bans). To address this challenge, I describe a collaborative project with Justin Gross, Philip Resnik, and Noah Smith. We advance a unified policy frames codebook, in which issue-specific frames (e.g., innocence) are nested within high-level categories of frames (e.g., fairness) that cross cut issues. Through manual annotation bolstered by supervised learning, we can track the relative use of different frame cues within a given issue over time and in an apples-to-apples way across issues. Preliminary findings suggest our work may help unlock the black box of framing, pointing to generalizable conditions under which we should expect to see different types of framing dynamics and framing effects.



*Proceedings of the ACL 2014 Workshop on Language Technologies and Computational Social Science*, page 71,
Baltimore, Maryland, USA, June 26, 2014. 

# "I Want to Talk About, Again, My Record On Energy ...": Modeling Agendas and Framing in Political Debates and Other Conversations

**Philip Resnik**
University of Maryland

## Abstract

Computational social science has been emerging over the last several years as a hotbed of interesting work, taking advantage of, to quote Lazer et al. (Science, v.323), "digital traces that can be compiled into comprehensive pictures of both individual and group behavior, with the potential to transform our understanding of our lives, organizations, and societies." Within that larger setting, I'm interested in how language is used to influence people, with an emphasis on computational modeling of agendas (who is most effectively directing attention, and toward what topics?), framing or "spin" (what underlying perspective does this language seek to encourage?), and sentiment (how does someone feel, as evidenced in the language they use)? These questions are particularly salient in political discourse. In this talk, I'll present recent work looking at political debates and other conversations using Bayesian models to capture relevant aspects of the conversational dynamics, as well as new methods for collecting people's reactions to speeches, debates, and other public conversations on a large scale.

This talk includes work done in collaboration with Jordan Boyd-Graber, Viet-An Nguyen, Deborah Cai, Amber Boydstun, Rebecca Glazier, Matthew Pietryka, Tim Jurka, and Kris Miler.



*Proceedings of the ACL 2014 Workshop on Language Technologies and Computational Social Science*, page 72,
Baltimore, Maryland, USA, June 26, 2014. 

# Author Index